CABINETMAKING AND MILLWORK STUDENT WORKBOOK

Dr. John L. Feirer

Keyed to the 1988 edition of
CABINETMAKING AND MILLWORK

GLENCOE/McGRAW-HILL
A Macmillan/McGraw-Hill Company
Mission Hills, California

Send all inquiries to:
Glencoe/McGraw-Hill
15319 Chatsworth Street
P.O. Box 9509
Mission Hills, CA 91395-9509

ISBN 0-02-675960-8

4 5 6 7   93 92 91 90

STUDENT INFORMATION

1. Name _____
            Last   First   Middle

2. Home address _____

3. Home phone number _____

4. Class _____

5. School attended last year _____

6. Homeroom _____

7. Father's name _____

8. Father's occupation _____

9. Father's work phone number _____

10. Mother's name _____

11. Mother's occupation _____

12. Mother's work phone number _____

13. Hobbies and outside interests _____

_____

14. Previous shop experience _____

_____

15. Name of family doctor _____

16. Doctor's address _____

17. Doctor's phone number _____

SAFETY PLEDGE

I pledge that I will follow all of the safety rules given in the book CABINETMAKING AND MILLWORK. I will also follow all of the shop regulations given by the instructor. I will not use a power tool without first securing the permission of the instructor. I will report all accidents to the instructor immediately, no matter how small they are. I will help to maintain a safe shop by tending to my business and by not bothering other students who are busy.

Date _____ Name _____

TABLE OF CONTENTS

TO THE TEACHER

This workbook is designed for use with the textbook CABINETMAKING AND MILLWORK. The units of this workbook are planned as teaching *and* learning aids.

Special effort has been made to integrate the best practices in language arts and mathematics with the activities that go on in the shop or laboratory. This workbook is planned so that the units can be used by students individually or in group activity.

Students can be asked to complete these units in one of several ways:

1. Each student may progress at his or her own rate of speed and complete the units as fast as possible.

2. The teacher may assign a lesson in the textbook as homework and then use the corresponding workbook unit for objective testing the next day.

3. Students may spend some time in supervised study covering the related information of the course.

4. Students can be assigned sections of the book for outside study and at the same time may be asked to complete the workbook units.

In addition to the individual units, this student workbook contains:

- a student information sheet
- a safety pledge for students to sign
- forms on which students can record their personnel assignments and the shop regulations
- a form on which students can record their workbook and classroom scores

TO THE STUDENT

This workbook will help you as you study CABINETMAKING AND MILLWORK. Each unit has the same number as the textbook unit it reviews. Completing the workbook units will help you recognize and remember the important facts in the textbook. It will also help you see how well you have understood the textbook.

To use this workbook, do the following:

1. Fill out the "Student Information" form (page 3). This sheet will help your teacher become better acquainted with you.

2. Read the safety pledge below the "Student Information" form. Sign the pledge to show that you will follow the safety rules.

3. In the space on page 9, make a list of the shop regulations that your teacher explains to you. You will be expected to follow those regulations.

4. Complete the workbook units as your teacher assigns them.

5. Keep a record of your scores, using the chart on pages 10 and 11.

You will find four different kinds of questions in this workbook. Here are samples of each kind. Study each one so that you will know the correct way to answer each question.

Completion: Study the sentence and decide what word would correctly complete the thought. Complete the sentence by writing the missing word in the blank at the left.

_____*Alaska*_____   1. SAMPLE: The largest state in the United States is _____ .

True or False: Read the statement carefully and decide whether it is true or false. Write True in the space if the statement is correct and False if it is wrong.

_____*True*_____   2. SAMPLE: Washington, D.C., is the capital of the United States.

Multiple Choice: Read the question and the possible answers. Write the letter of the correct answer in the answer blank.

___*C*___   3. SAMPLE: A state that is east of the Mississippi River is
        A. Colorado.
        B. Arizona.
        C. New York.
        D. North Dakota.

Matching: Match each item in the left-hand column to an item in the right-hand column. Write the letter of the correct choice in the answer blank to the left.

SAMPLE: Match each piece of equipment on the left with the sport in which it is used on the right by placing the letter of the correct answer in the blank.

___*A*___	4. goal posts	A. football
___*D*___	5. hoop	B. tennis
___*C*___	6. puck	C. hockey
___*B*___	7. racket	D. basketball

SAMPLE: Match the names of common eating utensils to the appropriate picture.

___*B*___   8. spoon

___*A*___   9. knife

___*C*___   10. fork

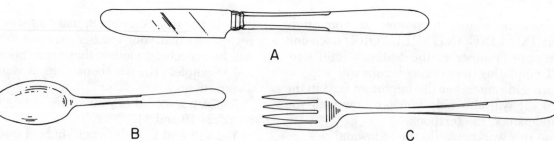

A

B   C

PERSONNEL AND CLEANUP ASSIGNMENTS

	Date		Job
From	_____ to _____		_____
From	_____ to _____		_____
From	_____ to _____		_____
From	_____ to _____		_____
From	_____ to _____		_____

SAFETY AND SHOP REGULATIONS

1. _____

2. _____

3. _____

4. _____

5. _____

6. _____

7. _____

8. _____

9. _____

10. _____

11. _____

12. _____

RECORD IN THE WOOD SHOP

Class Tests

No. 1 _____

No. 2 _____

No. 3 _____

No. 4 _____

No. 5 _____

No. 6 _____

No. 7 _____

No. 8 _____

Product Grades

1 _____
   Product   Grade

2 _____
   Product   Grade

3 _____
   Product   Grade

4 _____
   Product   Grade

5 _____
   Product   Grade

6 _____
   Product   Grade

7 _____
   Product   Grade

8 _____
   Product   Grade

Student Workbook Scores

UNIT	POSSIBLE SCORE	NUMBER CORRECT	UNIT	POSSIBLE SCORE	NUMBER CORRECT	UNIT	POSSIBLE SCORE	NUMBER CORRECT
1	16	_____	25	25	_____	49	21	_____
2	25	_____	26	33	_____	50	28	_____
3	32	_____	27	31	_____	51	29	_____
4	20	_____	28	28	_____	52	23	_____
5	38	_____	29	26	_____	53	22	_____
6	27	_____	30	24	_____	54	18	_____
7	22	_____	31	28	_____	55	17	_____
8	23	_____	32	29	_____	56	24	_____
9	24	_____	33	32	_____	57	36	_____
10	25	_____	34	34	_____	58	29	_____
11	30	_____	35	26	_____	59	22	_____
12	13	_____	36	30	_____	60	14	_____
13	15	_____	37	34	_____	61	15	_____
14	10	_____	38	34	_____	62	30	_____
15	21	_____	39	32	_____	63	23	_____
16	30	_____	40	33	_____	64	38	_____
17	14	_____	41	20	_____	65	35	_____
18	15	_____	42	33	_____	66	13	_____
19	21	_____	43	34	_____	67	17	_____
20	15	_____	44	30	_____	68	18	_____
21	22	_____	45	32	_____	69	15	_____
22	19	_____	46	33	_____	70	32	_____
23	19	_____	47	22	_____	71	21	_____
24	34	_____	48	27	_____	72	25	_____

Unit 1
CABINETMAKING—THE KEY TO ALL WOODWORKING

(Text pages 16-28)

_____ 1. Mass production has had little effect on cabinetmaking. (True or False)

_____ 2. Cabinetmaking is the largest skilled trade in the United States. (True or False)

_____ 3. The need for cabinetmaking skills is increasing. (True or False)

_____ 4. The Golden Age of furniture design was during the _____ century.

_____ 5. The "Big Four" designers of the Golden Age of furniture design were:
   A. Thomas Chippendale, Duncan Phyfe, Thomas Sheraton, and George Hepplewhite.
   B. Thomas Sheraton, John Adam, Samuel Adam, and Thomas Chippendale.
   C. Thomas Chippendale, George Hepplewhite, Thomas Sheraton, and the Adam brothers.
   D. The Adam brothers, Duncan Phyfe, Thomas Chippendale, and Louis XIV.

_____ 6. The only American designer-cabinetmaker for whom a style of furniture was named was _____ _____ .

Match the items on the left to the corresponding work of each listed in the column on the right.

_____ 7. finish carpenters

_____ 8. millwork plants

_____ 9. custom furniture makers

_____ 10. hardwood dimension plants

A. build doors, moldings, sash frames, etc.
B. build antique reproductions
C. fit, cut, and install doors, windows, paneling, etc.
D. build quality furniture parts in large quantities.

(Continued on next page)

11. Which of the following is *not* among the duties of a patternmaker?
    A. select proper types of wood
    B. study blueprints
    C. complete built-ins
    D. make the layout
    E. construct the pattern

12. A finish carpenter may either be an all-around skilled carpenter or may specialize in one particular area of work, such as installing plastic laminate or building kitchen cabinets. (True or False)

13. A person who uses wood and clay to make models for production is a
    A. wood technologist.
    B. patternmaker.
    C. molder.
    D. modelmaker.
    E. millwright.

14. Which of the following is *not* typical of the cabinetmaking field?
    A. It requires ability to use algebra.
    B. It is safe, involving no hazards.
    C. It requires only medium strength.
    D. Work is done mostly indoors and involves great variety.
    E. It requires at least two years of specialized vocational or technical training.

15. A cabinetmaker works only with hand tools. (True or False)

16. Most traditional woodworking occupations will not change with the increased use of plastics. (True or False)

Unit 2
FURNITURE DESIGNS

(Text pages 29-40)

_____ 1. What furniture style might have parts joined with wooden pegs rather than metal nails or screws?
   A. Spanish
   B. Duncan Phyfe
   C. Moorish
   D. Early American

_____ 2. The _____ was the most important piece of furniture for early American settlers.

_____ 3. _____ _____ was the author of a book that became the cabinetmaker's "bible."

Match the furniture designer on the left with the corresponding characteristics of his design on the right.

_____ 4. Duncan Phyfe   A. ball-and-claw foot
                                       B. straight-lined legs, squareback chairs
_____ 5. Thomas Chippendale   C. classic style adapted from ancient Rome; straight lines, simple curves
_____ 6. Thomas Sheraton   D. table with pedestal and three or four legs

_____ 7. Adam brothers

_____ 8. _____ is a style of leg shaped in a double curve, the top a convex line and the lower part a concave form.

_____ 9. Wood that is cut into decorative designs or patterns is called _____ .

_____ 10. Which of the following is *not* a common characteristic of Traditional furniture?
   A. mahogany
   B. extremely ornate
   C. carved details along edges of tops and on legs
   D. graceful, well-proportioned

_____ 11. As machines replaced hand tools in the making of furniture, the furniture became stronger and better proportioned. (True or False)

(Continued on next page)

12. Which of the following is *not* characteristic of Contemporary furniture?
    A. functional
    B. adaptable to many uses
    C. formal, with stiff lines and square angles
    D. natural finish

_____ 13. A style that combines both the Contemporary and Traditional is the _____ style.

_____ 14. The influence of the Orient can be seen in many pieces of Contemporary furniture. (True or False)

_____ 15. Which of the following is *not* characteristic of French Provincial furniture?
    A. cabriole leg
    B. carving, scrollwork, or fluting
    C. small black scratches on wood surface
    D. bronze claw at ends of legs

_____ 16. Furniture that is designed with small black scratches in the wood surface to imitate wear marks has a _____ finish.

_____ 17. Italian Provincial and French Provincial are quite similar styles. (True or False)

_____ 18. Most Italian Provincial chairs and cabinets have straight, tapered legs. (True or False)

_____ 19. Which of the following is *not* characteristic of the Spanish style?
    A. deeply carved geometric designs
    B. deeply carved cabriole legs
    C. use of wrought-iron metalwork, ceramics, and glass
    D. horseshoe shaped arch

Match the pictures on the following two pages to the proper furniture style or design.

_____ 20. Early American

_____ 21. Contemporary

_____ 22. Spanish

_____ 23. Italian Provincial

_____ 24. French Provincial

_____ 25. Traditional

(Continued on next page)

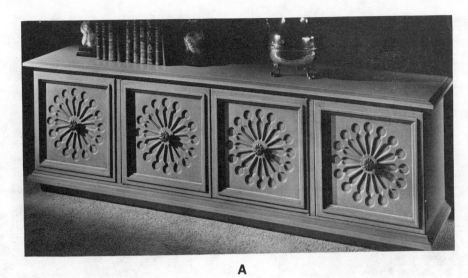

A

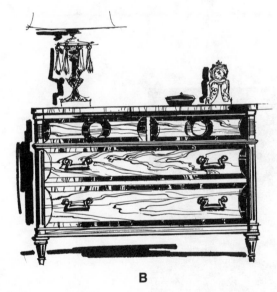

B

C

(Continued on next page)

D

E

F

Unit 3
DESIGNING FURNITURE AND CABINETS

(Text pages 41-57)

_____ 1. Good furniture and cabinet design should be determined by the need to live with things that are comfortable, convenient, pleasing in appearance, sturdy, and easy to maintain. (True or False)

_____ 2. A product is well designed only if it meets the need for which it was intended. (True or False)

_____ 3. The function of a chair is not important to its height. (True or False)

_____ 4. When making furniture in the school shop, you need to follow established styles or your project will be poorly designed. (True or False)

_____ 5. Plywood and non-wood materials are never used in quality furniture. (True or False)

_____ 6. Chairs which are joined with adhesives and dowels or corner blocks have inferior construction to those which are joined with mortise-and-tenon joints. (True or False)

_____ 7. Early American and French Provincial furniture often use ____ lines.

_____ 8. Contemporary furniture is largely made of ____ lines.

_____ 9. ____ is the three-dimensional appearance of an object.

(Continued on next page)

Match the names in the column below with the corresponding shapes.

_____ 10. ellipse

_____ 11. square

_____ 12. hexagon

_____ 13. triangle

_____ 14. circle

_____ 15. octagon

_____ 16. rectangle

_____ 17. diamond

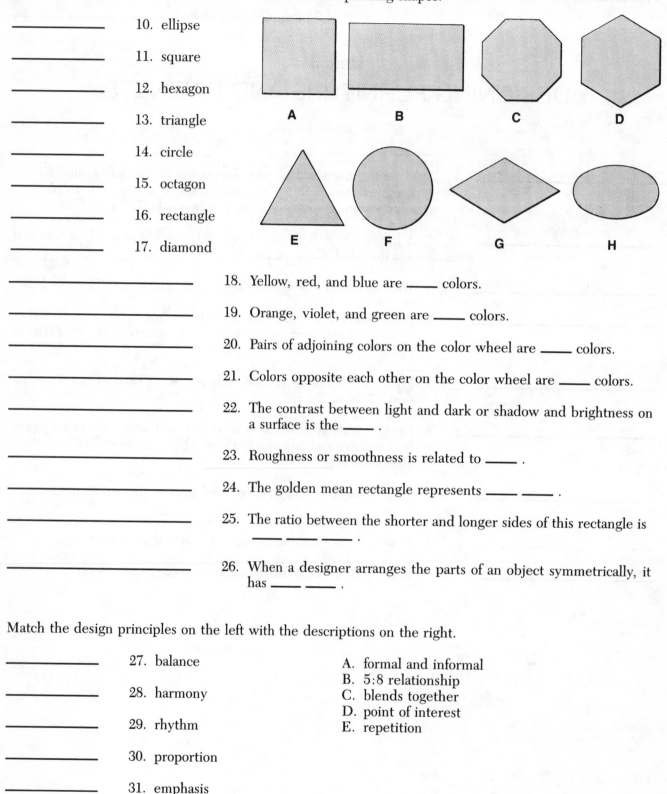

A   B   C   D

E   F   G   H

_____ 18. Yellow, red, and blue are _____ colors.

_____ 19. Orange, violet, and green are _____ colors.

_____ 20. Pairs of adjoining colors on the color wheel are _____ colors.

_____ 21. Colors opposite each other on the color wheel are _____ colors.

_____ 22. The contrast between light and dark or shadow and brightness on a surface is the _____ .

_____ 23. Roughness or smoothness is related to _____ .

_____ 24. The golden mean rectangle represents _____ _____ .

_____ 25. The ratio between the shorter and longer sides of this rectangle is ___ ___ .

_____ 26. When a designer arranges the parts of an object symmetrically, it has _____ _____ .

Match the design principles on the left with the descriptions on the right.

_____ 27. balance

_____ 28. harmony

_____ 29. rhythm

_____ 30. proportion

_____ 31. emphasis

A. formal and informal
B. 5:8 relationship
C. blends together
D. point of interest
E. repetition

_____ 32. Texture is more pronounced in Contemporary furniture than in most other styles. (True or False)

Unit 4
SAFETY AND HOUSEKEEPING

(Text pages 57-63)

_____   1. Industrial woodworking is one of the safest of all industrial activities. (True or False)

_____   2. Which of the following is *not* appropriate dress when using wood-working machines?
    A. apron
    B. tight-fitting long sleeves
    C. glasses
    D. non-metal watch
    E. All of the above are inappropriate.

_____   3. One cannot be expected to keep the work area free of such things as oil, wood scraps, and sawdust piles. (True or False)

_____   4. Never try to pull stock through a machine. (True or False)

_____   5. Sharp tools are safer than dull tools. (True or False)

_____   6. When it is necessary to cut a small piece of wood, you should
    A. ask someone else to hold the wood while you carefully cut it.
    B. wear gloves to help protect your fingers.
    C. clamp the wood in a vise.
    D. carefully turn the stock so the cutting edge moves toward your hand as you cut.

_____   7. Portable tools with fiberglass housings help eliminate much of the danger of shock. (True or False)

_____   8. When the guard on a stationary machine makes cutting impossible, you should
    A. not perform the cutting operation.
    B. ask your instructor to help you make a different type of guard that will work.
    C. try a different machine.
    D. use a clamping device and/or push stick.

_____   9. Planning your work before you begin can eliminate much potential danger. (True or False)

_____   10. Feed the stock into the machine immediately after turning it on. (True or False)

(Continued on next page)

_____ 11. Adjust the machine only after it has reached full speed. (True or False)

_____ 12. Always wear ____ when grinding, turning, and drilling.

_____ 13. A good ____ system is necessary for both fire control and health reasons.

_____ 14. A ____ ____ fire involves inflammable liquids such as alcohol, paint, or lacquer thinner.

_____ 15. A ____ ____ fire involves only ordinary combustible material such as wood chips or paper.

_____ 16. A ____ ____ fire involves electrical equipment.

_____ 17. Which type of extinguisher should *not* be used for an electrical fire?
    A. carbon dioxide
    B. foam
    C. vaporizing liquid
    D. dry chemical

_____ 18. Water or substances containing water should never be used on class A fires. (True or False)

_____ 19. If you have a fire involving paint thinner, which of the following extinguishers would you use?
    A. soda-acid
    B. water pump
    C. carbon dioxide
    D. none of the above

_____ 20. There is no need to report minor injuries such as scratches and splinters. (True or False)

Unit 5
WOOD—ITS NATURE AND PROPERTIES

(Text pages 66-80)

_____   1. The tiny cells of wood are held together by ____ .

Match the parts of the tree on the left with the descriptions on the right.

_____   2. crown

_____   3. outer bark

_____   4. bast

_____   5. cambium

_____   6. xylem

_____   7. sapwood

_____   8. heartwood

_____   9. pith

_____   10. ray cells

_____   11. roots

_____   12. trunk

A. living layer between bark and wood
B. the center of the tree; the first growth
C. the wood of the tree; used for lumber
D. inactive, dark material
E. inner bark; also called phloem
F. horizontal passageways for food
G. the twigs and leaves
H. dead, corky part that protects tree from fire, insects, and disease
I. carries water and nutrients from roots to leaves
J. absorb water, minerals, and nitrogen; anchor the tree
K. produces the bulk of useful wood; supports the crown

_____   13. Some hardwoods are softer than some softwoods. (True or False)

_____   14. Softwoods are those that come from ____ .

_____   15. Hardwoods are cut from ____ trees.

_____   16. Springwood and summerwood combined make up the ____ ____ .

_____   17. The arrangement of cells in wood when it is cut end to end determines the ____ .

_____   18. The pattern produced by growth rings, rays, knots, and deviations from regular grain is called the ____ of wood.

(Continued on next page)

_____   19. Woods that have a high specific gravity are stronger and harder than those of low rating. (True or False)

_____   20. The ability of wood to resist denting is called
                         A. specific gravity.
                         B. density.
                         C. compression strength.
                         D. hardness.

Match the method of cutting on the left to the description on the right.

_____   21. plain-sawed   A. softwood squared and sawed lengthwise
                                                       B. softwood sawed so that its rings form 45° to 90°
_____   22. flat-grained   angles with surface
                                                       C. hardwood squared and sawed lengthwise
_____   23. quarter-sawed   D. hardwood sawed so that its rings form 45° to 90°
                                                          angles with surface
_____   24. edge-grained

_____   25. _____ lumber has less tendency to warp, shrink, and swell and pro-
                         vides a more durable surface.

_____   26. _____ lumber is cheaper, easier to kiln dry, and produces greater
                         widths, but it has a high tendency to shrink and warp.

Match the lumber defects on the left with the descriptions on the right.

_____   27. knot   A. lengthwise separation of the wood
                                                       B. areas of disintegrated wood
_____   28. pith   C. any variation from a true or plane surface
                                                       D. bark left on a board
_____   29. peck   E. portion of a branch or limb
                                                       F. small soft core in center of log
_____   30. pocket   G. opening between growth rings
                                                       H. any unsurfaced area
_____   31. skip

_____   32. warp

_____   33. wane

_____   34. shake

Match the kinds of warp with the drawings.

_____   35. bow

_____   36. crook

_____   37. twist

_____   38. cup

Unit 6
KINDS OF WOODS

(Text pages 80-101)

_____   1. If you have trouble identifying a particular wood, you can send it to the ____ ____ ____ .

_____   2. Most furniture woods are hardwoods. (True or False)

_____   3. Douglas-fir is especially good for food containers because it has no odor. (True or False)

_____   4. Which of the following softwoods is moderately hard?
     A. ponderosa pine
     B. Sitka spruce
     C. western larch
     D. sugar pine

_____   5. All softwoods have only low to moderate decay resistance. (True or False)

Match the type of wood on the left with the product for which it is commonly used.

_____   6. shortleaf pine   A. barrels and kegs
                                       B. boats

_____   7. sugar pine   C. bushel baskets
                                       D. telephone poles

_____   8. redwood   E. outdoor furniture
                                       F. baseball bats

_____   9. white ash   G. foundry patterns
                                       H. spools, bobbins, and furniture

_____   10. American basswood   I. core material for furniture

_____   11. yellow birch

_____   12. rock elm

_____   13. American elm

_____   14. true mahogany

_____   15. A wood often confused with hickory is ____ ____ .

(Continued on next page)

_____

16. Which of the following hardwoods is *not* soft?
    A. basswood
    B. beech
    C. cottonwood
    D. yellow poplar

_____

17. A hardwood especially suitable for food containers is _____ .

_____

18. Which of the following is *not* true of yellow birch?
    A. widely used in furniture industry
    B. very large shrinkage
    C. difficult to work with hand tools
    D. high in decay resistance

_____

19. _____ _____ is often used in Traditional furniture such as Chippendale.

_____

20. Of all commercial hardwoods, _____ combines the best qualities of toughness, hardness, and stiffness.

_____

21. _____ _____ is very resistant to wear and is often used on dance floors and bowling alleys.

_____

22. A wood that sometimes has curly, wavy, or bird's-eye grain is _____ _____ .

_____

23. The leading wood for boat and ship construction is _____ _____ .

_____

24. An important flooring wood for residences is _____ _____ .

_____

25. A wood often used in combination with or in place of walnut is _____ .

_____

26. A wood particularly suitable for making gunstocks is _____ _____ .

_____

27. Which of the following is *not* noted for its bending qualities?
    A. white ash
    B. American elm
    C. black cherry
    D. yellow poplar

Unit 7
FINE FURNITURE WOODS

(Text pages 101-116)

_____   1. Which of the following is *not* true of walnut?
   A. endless variety of figures
   B. takes oiled finishes better than any other wood
   C. in plentiful supply
   D. varies considerably in color

_____   2. Wood cut from the _____ of the tree often has a beautiful swirled figure.

_____   3. A large wartlike growth on a tree that provides a prized grain pattern is called a _____ .

_____   4. The stump of a tree does not have wood suitable for quality furniture. (True or False)

_____   5. Which of the following is *not* true of mahogany?
   A. takes flat, rubbed oil finishes as readily as it takes hard, glossy oil finishes
   B. provides some of the broadest boards
   C. expensive
   D. softer than many hardwoods

_____   6. Thomas Chippendale introduced mahogany's familiar _____ finish.

_____   7. There is little waste to mahogany lumber. (True or False)

_____   8. Which of the following is *not* true of cherry?
   A. one of the earliest furniture woods
   B. close-grained
   C. little waste in turning logs to lumber
   D. expensive

_____   9. The finish most often associated with cherry furniture is _____ .

_____   10. Which of the following woods is *not* commonly used for Early American style furniture?
   A. maple
   B. birch
   C. cherry
   D. walnut

(Continued on next page)

_____ 11. Birch and maple have very similar color and grain. (True or False)

_____ 12. Which of the following is *not* true of maple?
   A. acoustical properties
   B. glues up easily
   C. hard
   D. fine, even texture

_____ 13. Which of the following is *not* true of yellow birch?
   A. close, compact grain
   B. widely used for doors, floors, and wall paneling
   C. dense and hard
   D. often called "mountain mahogany"
   E. has swirl figure when quarter-sawed

_____ 14. What wood is commonly used in combination with walnut to make parquet floors?

_____ 15. No filler is needed when working with oak. (True or False)

_____ 16. Products made of oak are highly resistant to changes of weather. (True or False)

_____ 17. Oak furniture demands a high degree of care. (True or False)

_____ 18. The wood that is so dense it will not float and feels oily to the touch is ____ .

_____ 19. A very expensive wood from Sri Lanka that has deep luster and is highly figured is ____ .

_____ 20. A wood with dark stripes on a light background is ____ .

_____ 21. A wood from Brazil and India that has a pattern streaked with dark-brown or black pigment and has a heavy residue of oil is ____ .

_____ 22. A wood sometimes misnamed "white mahogany" is ____ .

Unit 8
PLYWOOD

(Text pages 116-129)

_____   1. As much as 90 per cent of the wood used in fine furniture today is plywood. (True or False)

_____   2. Which of the following is *not* among the advantages plywood has over solid wood?
A. The natural beauty of the wood can be shown to best advantage.
B. It is stronger with the grain.
C. Splitting is reduced.
D. Warping is reduced.

_____   3. ____ plywood contains a core of narrow, sawed-lumber strips with crossbands and face veneer glued on both sides.

_____   4. ____ plywood is made by gluing three, five, seven, or nine plies of thin veneer.

_____   5. Balanced construction means
A. all plies are the same type of wood.
B. adjoining plies are at right angles to each other.
C. all plies are arranged in pairs, one on either side of the core.
D. there are an even number of plies.

_____   6. The purpose of balanced construction is to add strength to the wood. (True or False)

Match the grades of hardwood plywood on the left with the description on the right.

_____   7. good
_____   8. sound
_____   9. utility
_____   10. premium

A. face veneers carefully matched for color and grain
B. used for a natural finish; face veneers do not need to be precisely matched
C. smooth surface; is usually painted
D. may have some discoloration and small knot-holes

_____   11. Construction and industrial plywood is made only from softwoods. (True or False)

_____   12. Construction and industrial plywood has ____ -core construction.

(Continued on next page)

_____ 13. Which of the following would be the best grade of plywood?
A. A-A
B. A-B
C. N-A
D. N-N

Match the following types of plywood with the proper description.

_____ 14. flexwood   A. composition panel with exterior of hardboard, interior of plywood

_____ 15. striated plywood   B. tough, smooth surface; two more plies than regular plywood

_____ 16. plyron   C. combed surface for unusual texture
                       D. grain pattern accentuated to produce a three-dimensional look
_____ 17. ripplewood plywood
                       E. wood veneer fastened to special cloth backing
_____ 18. fiberply

_____ 19. When hand sawing plywood, place the good face ____ .

_____ 20. When cutting plywood with a portable power saw, place the good face ____ .

_____ 21. When planing plywood,
A. work from the center toward each edge.
B. work from one edge across to the other edge.
C. work from both ends toward the center.
D. the edges will splinter, so you should not attempt to plane plywood.

_____ 22. Nails and screws do not hold well in the edge of plywood. (True or False)

_____ 23. When building with plywood, the best joint for corners is the ____ joint.

Unit 9
HARDBOARD AND PARTICLE BOARD

(Text pages 129-139)

_____ 1. Hardboard is made from refined wood _____ .

_____ 2. The label S2S on hardboard means that
   A. both sides have been surface planed.
   B. it is suitable for both exterior and interior use.
   C. both sides are smooth.
   D. it is service strength hardboard.

Match the types of hardboard on the left with the descriptions on the right.

_____ 3. acoustical   A. excellent for storage or display purposes
                                     B. made to simulate other materials
_____ 4. service   C. for sound control
                                     D. furniture and cabinetwork
_____ 5. perforated   E. used where low weight is an advantage

_____ 6. embossed

_____ 7. standard

_____ 8. After arriving from the lumberyard, hardwood sheets need at least 24 hours to adjust to their new environment before being used. (True or False)

_____ 9. Before attaching hardboard to a bathroom wall, the panels should be exposed for a long time to damp air or have water scrubbed into the back. (True or False)

_____ 10. Hardboard requires special tools and care when machining and drilling. (True or False)

_____ 11. Hardboard cannot be bent. (True or False)

_____ 12. Hardboard ¼″ thick has excellent screw-holding strength for attaching hinges. (True or False)

_____ 13. Hardboard will take almost any type of finish. (True or False)

_____ 14. Particle board is made from wood particles combined with a(n) _____ .

(Continued on next page)

_____

15. _____ is a high-quality particle board in which the flakes are carefully cut with the grain to precise thickness and length.

_____

16. Single-layer particle board is best suited for applying plastic laminates. (True or False)

_____

17. Hardboard and particle board are equal in hardness. (True or False)

_____

18. Particle board can be sawed and machined easily with standard woodworking tools and machines. (True or False)

_____

19. It is not necessary to add crossbands when applying veneers to particle board. (True or False)

_____

20. The nail-holding power of particle board is equal to that of standard wood. (True or False)

_____

21. The largest finishing nail that should be used on particle board is _____ .

_____

22. When fastening particle board _____ _____ screws should be used for best holding power.

_____

23. Most particle board is used for _____ _____ .

_____

24. Particle board needs to be filled and sealed before it can be painted. (True or False)

Unit 10
MILLWORK, INCLUDING MOLDING

(Text pages 139-147)

_____   1. Stock millwork is mass-produced. (True or False)

Match the type of window on the left with the appropriate picture.

_____   2. casement

_____   3. awning

_____   4. horizontal sliding

_____   5. double hung

_____   6. hopper

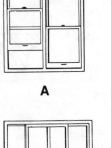
A

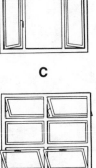
C

E

B

D

Match the type of molding on the left with the description on the right.

_____   7. cove

_____   8. crown

_____   9. casing

_____   10. stool

_____   11. quarter round

_____   12. baluster

_____   13. batten

_____   14. stop

_____   15. mullion

A. upright in railings
B. inside of corner trim
C. inside of sloping window sill
D. concave face, used same as crown
E. break between wall and ceiling
F. decorative trim between windows in a series
G. covers cracks between boards in paneling and siding
H. trim for doors and windows
I. holds window sash in place; makes snug joints

_____   16. The function of molding is purely decorative. (True or False)

(Continued on next page)

Match the pictures on the right to the type of molding on the left.

_____ 17. crown

_____ 18. picture molding

_____ 19. quarter round

_____ 20. cove

_____ 21. base

_____ 22. base shoe

_____ 23. stop

_____ 24. mullion

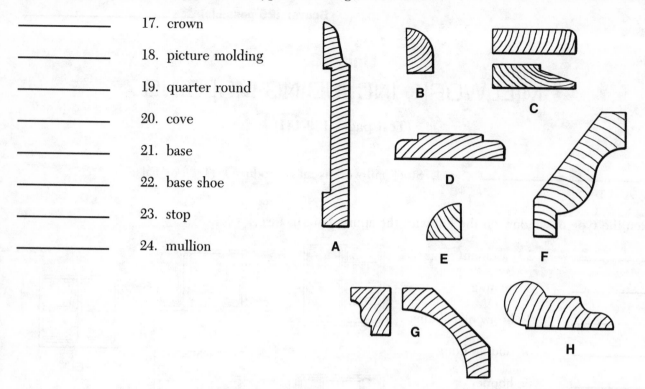

_____ 25. Molding can change a simple piece of casework into furniture with definite style. (True or False)

Unit 11
FASTENERS

(Text pages 147-162)

_____ 1. _____ nails are usually used for cabinet work trim.

_____ 2. _____ nails are used for window and door frames, cornices, and corner boards.

_____ 3. Length of nails is indicated by the _____ system.

_____ 4. Diameter of nails is indicated by the _____ _____ system.

_____ 5. The lower the gage number, the bigger the nail. (True or False)

_____ 6. A pound of 4d finishing nails will have the same number of nails as a pound of 4d casing nails. (True or False)

_____ 7. A _____ _____ is a tool used to sink the head of a nail below the surface.

_____ 8. Driving the nail in at a 30-degree angle to join end grain to face grain is called _____ .

_____ 9. No special technique is needed to nail hardwood. (True or False)

_____ 10. In nailing solid lumber a few staggered nails provide greater strength than several nails in a straight row. (True or False)

Name the common screw heads shown.

_____ 11.

_____ 12.

_____ 13.

11   **12**   **13**

(Continued on next page)

_____ 14. The difference between wood screws and sheet metal screws is that
 A. sheet metal screws have different heads.
 B. sheet metal screws are not pointed at the end.
 C. sheet metal screws are threaded their entire length.
 D. sheet metal screws are made of stronger metal.

Match the tools on the left with the descriptions on the right.

_____ 15. screw-mate counterbore

_____ 16. Phillips screwdriver

_____ 17. spiral-type screwdriver

_____ 18. screw-mate drill and countersink

_____ 19. 82-degree countersink

_____ 20. offset screwdriver

A. to be used in close quarters
B. for installing flathead screws that are to be flush with surface
C. will drill, countersink, make shank clearance, and make pilot hole all at once
D. for recessed-head screws
E. will drill holes for wood plugs
F. has three bits for plain screws, one for Phillips

_____ 21. The ____ hole is for the threadless portion of a wood screw.

_____ 22. The ____ hole is for the part that is threaded.

_____ 23. When fastening two pieces of wood, ____ of the screw's length should extend into the second piece.
 A. one-half
 B. one-third
 C. two-thirds
 D. three-fourths

_____ 24. Steel screws should always be used with oak. (True or False)

Match the fasteners on the left with the descriptions on the right.

_____ 25. molly screw

_____ 26. toggle bolt

_____ 27. anchor bolt

_____ 28. masonry nail

_____ 29. rawl plug

A. made of hardened steel with knurled body
B. made of fiber and used with wood, sheet metal, or lag screws
C. anchor shank completely fills the hole in the wall
D. made with spring head or solid head
E. has base attached to wall with adhesive

_____ 30. Clamp nails, chevrons, and corrugated fasteners are commonly used to hold ____ ____ .

Unit 12
HARDWARE

(Text pages 162-166)

_____   1. You should not buy the hardware for a project before building it. (True or False)

_____   2. There are styles of hardware to go along with the different styles of furniture. (True or False)

Match the furniture or furniture parts on the left with the hardware most commonly used for them on the right.

_____   3. rolling door

_____   4. lip door

_____   5. drop door

_____   6. flush door

_____   7. overlapping door

_____   8. cabinet interior

_____   9. drawer

_____   10. screen

_____   11. All hardware is made of metal. (True or False)

A. double-action
B. surface, concealed, or semi-concealed hinge
C. pivot hinge
D. handles and a metal track
E. continuous or piano hinge
F. shelf supports
G. slides, pulls, and locks
H. butt hinge

Identify the type of hinge shown in each picture.

_____   12.

_____   13.

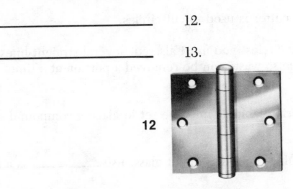

12

13

Unit 13
GLASS AND MIRRORS

(Text pages 166-172)

_____ 1. It is usually the responsibility of the cabinetmaker to install glass and mirrors. (True or False)

_____ 2. The glass most commonly used in cabinets is _____ glass.

_____ 3. Double-strength glass is twice as thick as single-strength glass. (True or False)

_____ 4. The highest-quality sheet glass is rated _____ .

_____ 5. _____ glass is a heavy sheet glass sometimes substituted for plate glass.

_____ 6. Highest quality window glass is completely free of defects. (True or False)

_____ 7. _____ glass goes through a grinding and polishing process.

_____ 8. Mirrors are made from highest-quality _____ glass.

_____ 9. Only window glass can be bent. (True or False)

_____ 10. Cutting a sharp, even groove in glass is called _____ .

_____ 11. After the cut has been made, the waste piece
A. will automatically fall after a slight tap.
B. should be removed with a quick upward snap.
C. should be carefully pulled away with a slow, level, sideways movement.
D. should be removed with a quick downward snap.

_____ 12. A _____ glass cutter is used to cut circles.

_____ 13. When cutting circles, you must also cut several straight lines away from the circle so waste can be removed a portion at a time. (True or False)

_____ 14. Glass for interior cabinets must be set in glazing compound. (True or False)

_____ 15. When smoothing the edges of cut glass, use _____ _____ as a lubricant.

Unit 14
MACHINE-MADE CANE WEBBING

(Text pages 172-174)

_____   1. Cane is made by cutting ____ into thin strips.
    A. bamboo shoots
    B. wild reeds
    C. rattan stems
    D. bullrushes

_____   2. Cane is most commonly used on
    A. Traditional furniture.
    B. Spanish furniture.
    C. Italian Provincial furniture.
    D. Contemporary furniture.

_____   3. On a finished piece of furniture the cane is held in place by a ____ ____ .

_____   4. It is usually unnecessary to make a pattern to use when cutting cane. (True or False)

_____   5. The cane should be cut
    A. one inch smaller than the opening it is to cover because it will stretch.
    B. the same size as the opening it is to cover.
    C. after it has soaked in water.
    D. one inch larger than the actual opening.
    E. only after it has been fitted into the grooves of the frame.

_____   6. Cut or rout a groove about ____ wide around the opening to be covered.

_____   7. Soak the cane in warm water before putting it in the frame in order to
    A. shrink it.
    B. bring out the natural color.
    C. make it pliable.
    D. remove any dirt from between the weaves.

_____   8. When placing the wedges to temporarily hold the cane in the grooves, start at the part closest to you. (True or False)

_____   9. A small amount of ____ ____ glue should be placed in the grooves.

_____   10. After installing the cane, a ____ is glued on to cover the wood holding the cane in place.

Unit 15
ORDERING LUMBER AND OTHER MATERIALS

(Text pages 174-185)

_____ 1. A board measuring 2″ x 6″ x 24″ contains ____ board feet.

_____ 2. A 2″ x 4″ piece that is 12′ long contains ____ board feet.

_____ 3. Ten pieces of lumber 1″ x 3″ x 12′ equal ____ board feet.

_____ 4. Plywood and hardboard are sold by the ____ ____ .

_____ 5. Molding, trim, and dowel rod are sold by the ____ ____ .

_____ 6. Another term for nominal size is ____ size.

_____ 7. Another term for dressed lumber is ____ lumber.

_____ 8. Lumber sizes are based on rough, green dimensions. (True or False)

Identify these commonly used lumber abbreviations.

_____ 9. DIM

_____ 10. S2S

_____ 11. KD

_____ 12. HDWD

_____ 13. RDM

_____ 14. RGH

_____ 15. SEL

_____ 16. S1S1E

_____ 17. M

_____ 18. ____ lumber is softwood lumber of those grades, sizes, and patterns intended for ordinary construction and general building purposes.

_____ 19. Quality can vary greatly within the same grade of lumber. (True or False)

_____ 20. The best grade of hardwood is ____ .

_____ 21. ____ is used to find the amount of board feet in a pile of lumber.

Unit 16
READING PRINTS AND MAKING SKETCHES

(Text pages 185-204)

_____   1. Blueprints are usually used in furniture making and interior cabi-
                                 network. (True or False)

_____   2. A(n) ____ line is a very light line used to "block in" an object.

_____   3. A(n) ____ line is a heavy line used to outline the exterior shape of
                                 a part, showing the outstanding features.

Name the lines shown in the illustrations.

_____   4.

_____   5.

_____   6.

_____   7.

_____   8.

_____   9.

_____   10.

_____   11.

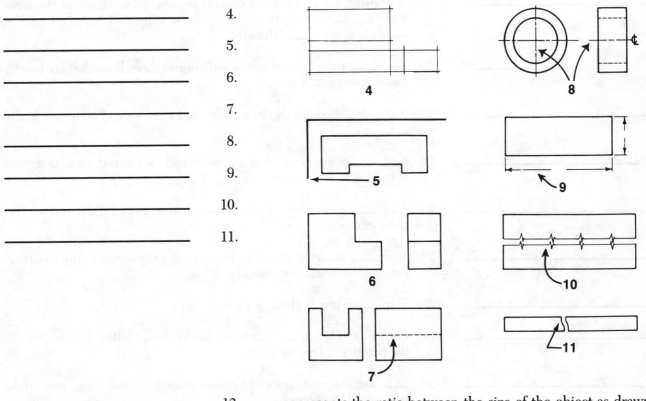

_____   12. ____ represents the ratio between the size of the object as drawn
                                  and its actual size.

_____   13. A life-size drawing is called a(n) ____ drawing.

(Continued on next page)

41

Identify these symbols.

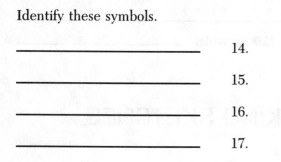

_____ 14.

_____ 15.

_____ 16.

_____ 17.

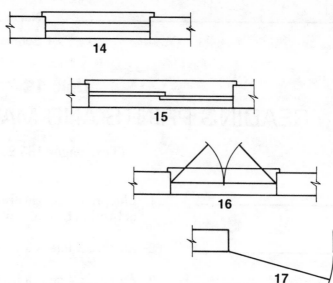

_____ 18. A drawing that shows the finished appearance of an object is a(n) _____ drawing.

_____ 19. A drawing for rectangular objects in which the shape of the front surface is shown in exact scale and the sides and top slant back at an angle is a(n) _____ drawing.

_____ 20. A(n) _____ drawing is constructed around three lines that are exactly 120 degrees apart.

_____ 21. A drawing showing the front, top, and right side of an object is a(n) _____ _____ .

_____ 22. A(n) _____ view is needed when there is a slanted view that does not show in true shape.

_____ 23. A(n) _____ view shows the interior of an object as if the surface had been cut away.

_____ 24. A(n) _____ drawing shows individual parts separated so the construction can be seen more clearly.

_____ 25. The _____ view is the top view.

_____ 26. Cabinet and furniture drawings should always follow standard drafting practice. (True or False)

_____ 27. _____ are external views of a house made from the front, rear, right side, and left side.

_____ 28. _____ are written descriptive material that accompany the plans.

_____ 29. In architectural drawings, the _____ drawings show a specific part of the house that was not made clear on the general plans.

_____ 30. In making a sketch, the most important thing is accuracy of _____ .

Unit 17
MATERIAL NEEDS, PLANNING, AND ESTIMATING

(Text pages 205-213)

_____   1. The procedure for making a bill of materials is called ____ ____ .

_____   2. Which of the following is *not* included on a bill of materials?
   A. drawing of the project
   B. name of each part
   C. finish size in thickness, width, and length
   D. type of wood needed

_____   3. The rough or cut-out size is on a ____ list.

_____   4. The finish thickness and the rough thickness for plywood are the same. (True or False)

_____   5. The actual or finish size of a piece is also called the ____ size.

_____   6. The ____ size is the size that must be cut from the standard piece of lumber.

_____   7. On a bill of materials, write thickness and width in inches and fractions of inches, and write length in feet and fractions of feet. (True or False)

_____   8. If a bill of materials calls for several pieces to be made from ¾″ pine, it is a good idea to make a ____ ____ to save waste.

_____   9. Which of the following does *not* need to be included on a lumber and materials order?
   A. total cost
   B. number of board, square, or linear feet
   C. sizes in thickness, width, and length
   D. fittings and finishing materials

_____   10. In industry, a(n) ____ makes the detail drawings and stock bills.

_____   11. The plan that details the steps or operations to complete a project is a(n) ____ ____ ____ .

(Continued on next page)

_____   12. Furniture plants use ____ ____ to list the steps or operations for each part of a product.

_____   13. Which of the following is *not* considered when estimating the total cost of producing a piece of furniture?
A. materials
B. labor
C. consumer demand
D. profit

_____   14. ____ refers to the fixed costs of running a business, such as utilities and machines.

Unit 18
MAKING A LAYOUT

(Text pages 213-224)

Name the parts of the steel square in the illustration.

_____   1.

_____   2.

_____   3.

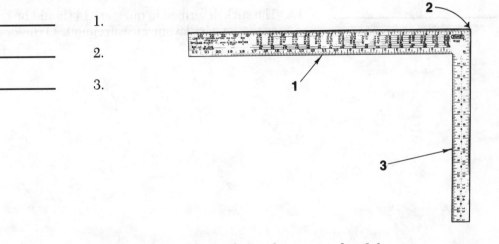

_____   4. The picture above shows the _____ side of the square.

_____   5. The opposite side of the picture above would be the _____ side.

_____   6. The _____ are the inch divisions and the graduations in fractions of an inch found on the outer and inner edges of the square.

_____   7. The _____ _____ is used for laying out lines to cut an eight-sided figure.

_____   8. The _____ _____ is found along the center of the tongue back.

_____   9. For making braces when the horizontal and vertical are not the same, use the _____ _____ .

_____   10. You have a 5½" wide board. You lay the rule at an angle across the board so that the end of the rule is at one edge of the board and the 6" mark is at the other edge. You mark the board at each inch mark. You are
A. going to make one-inch strips.
B. making a line tangent.
C. laying out a brace.
D. dividing the board into equal parts.

(Continued on next page)

_____ 11. Whenever anything round is shown in isometric, draw a(n) _____ .

_____ 12. If the original squares are ¼″ in size and the enlarged squares are 2″ in size, the full-size pattern will be _____ times larger than the original.

_____ 13. When many parts of the same size and shape are used, it is a good idea to make a _____ of plywood or sheet metal as a pattern.

_____ 14. In a _____ _____ _____ _____ , full-size measurements for height, width, and depth are all marked on a stick, with one dimension on each side of the stick.

_____ 15. The stick described in question 14 should be exactly the same length as the longest layout measurement. (True or False)

Unit 19
LAYOUT, MEASURING, AND CHECKING DEVICES

(Text pages 228-229)

_____   1. The bench rule can be used as both a measuring device and a straightedge. (True or False)

_____   2. When using a steel tape for inside measurement, add _____ inches to the reading on the blade.

Identify the tools in the illustrations.

_____   3.

_____   4.

_____   5.

_____   6.

_____   7.

_____   8.

_____   9.

_____   10.

_____   11.

_____   12.

_____   13.

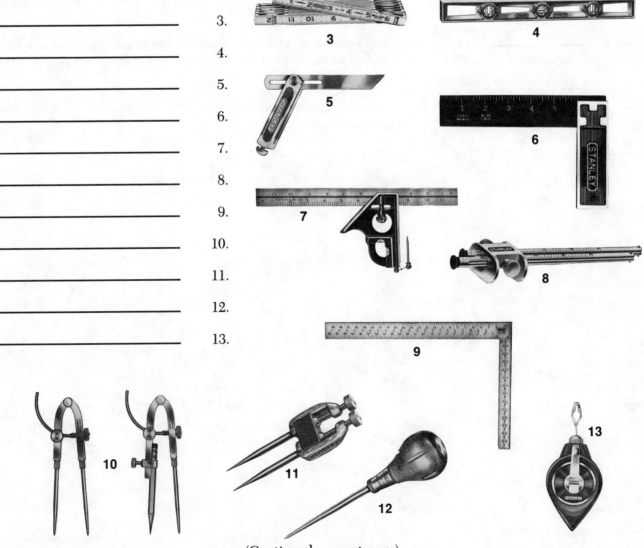

(Continued on next page)

_____   14. To measure distances of less than two feet with a zig-zag rule, the rule should lie flat on the stock. (True or False)

_____   15. Which of the following is the combination square *not* used for?
                        A. to test a level or plumb surface
                        B. to mark and test a 45-degree miter
                        C. to lay out rafters
                        D. to check inside squareness

_____   16. To measure or transfer an angle between 0 and 180 degrees, use a(n) ___ ___ ___ .

_____   17. A tool with two metal legs, one of which can be replaced with a pencil, and is used to lay out circles and arcs is a(n) ___ .

_____   18. A pointed metal tool used to scribe a line or locate a point, such as marking the center of holes to be drilled or bored, is a(n) ___ ___ .

_____   19. A tool used to mark a line parallel to the grain of the wood is the ___ ___ .

_____   20. A tool consisting of two metal points that can be fastened to a long bar of wood or metal to lay out distances between two points is the ___ ___ .

_____   21. A device that can be hung from a string to establish a vertical line is a(n) ___ ___ .

Unit 20
SAWING TOOLS

(Text pages 230-231)

Identify each type of saw in the illustrations.

_____   1.

_____   2.

_____   3.

_____   4.

_____   5.

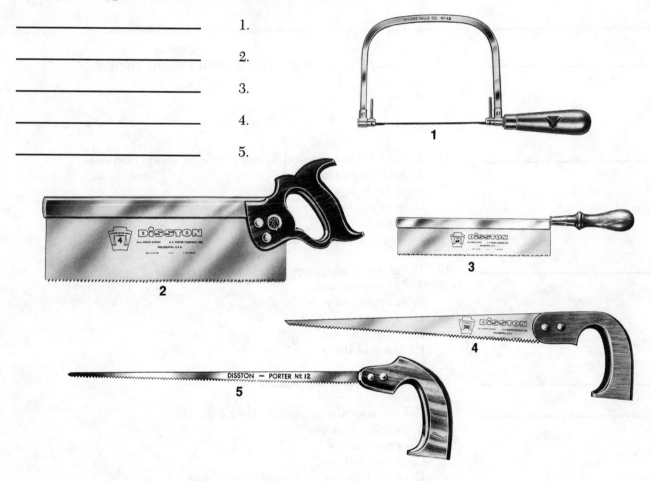

6. A back saw is actually a type of rip saw. (True or False)

7. The type of saw used in a miter box is
   A. a rip saw.
   B. a back saw.
   C. a dovetail saw.
   D. a 4 point crosscut saw.
   E. none of the above.

(Continued on next page)

8. To cut with the grain, use
    A. a coping saw.
    B. a rip saw.
    C. a crosscut saw.
    D. a dovetail saw.
    E. none of the above.

9. To cut a board across the grain, use a _____ saw.

10. A _____ point saw is good for general purpose crosscutting.
    A. 4
    B. 6
    C. 10
    D. 12
    E. 15

11. A _____ point saw is good for general purpose ripping.
    A. 8
    B. 5½
    C. 10½
    D. 12

12. A taper blade saw used to cut gentle or inside curves is
    A. a coping saw.
    B. a keyhole saw.
    C. a compass saw.
    D. a jig saw.
    E. none of the above.

13. To cut small openings and do fine work, use
    A. a compass saw.
    B. a coping saw.
    C. a dovetail saw.
    D. a keyhole saw.
    E. none of the above

14. For scroll work, use a _____ saw.

15. For the smoothest possible joint cuts, use
    A. a miter box saw.
    B. a coping saw.
    C. a dovetail saw.
    D. a keyhole saw.
    E. none of the above

Unit 21
EDGE-CUTTING TOOLS

(Text pages 231-233)

Identify each type of plane shown.

_____ 1.

_____ 2.

_____ 3.

_____ 4.

_____ 5.

_____ 6.

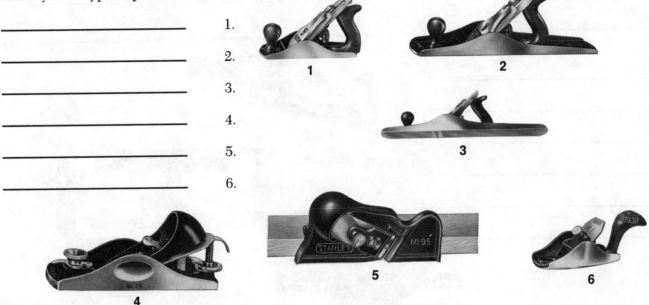

Match the type of plane to the job for which it is usually used.

_____ 7. model-maker's plane
_____ 8. router plane
_____ 9. block plane
_____ 10. jointer plane
_____ 11. jack plane

A. end grain
B. edges of doors
C. concave, curved surfaces
D. rough surface where chip should be coarse
E. bottom of grooves and dadoes

_____ 12. To cut grooves or shape irregular openings, use a ____ .

_____ 13. To form irregularly shaped objects, use a ____ .

(Continued on next page)

_____ 14. To cut and trim veneer, hardboard, and particle board, use a
  A. draw knife.
  B. surform tool.
  C. spokeshave.
  D. utility knife.

_____ 15. When a planing job requires extreme accuracy, use a
  A. model-maker's plane.
  B. jointer plane.
  C. rabbet plane.
  D. block plane.

_____ 16. To remove much material in a short time, use a(n) ____ ____ .

Identify the tools shown.

_____ 17.

_____ 18.

_____ 19.

_____ 20.

_____ 21.

_____ 22.

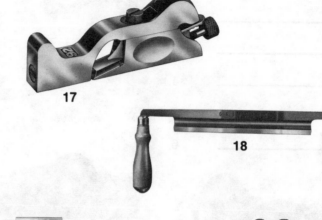
17

18

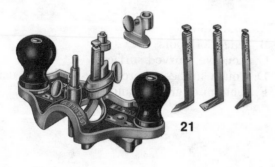
19
STANLEY

20

21

22

Unit 22
DRILLING AND BORING TOOLS

(Text pages 234-235)

Identify the tools shown.

_____ 1.

_____ 2.

_____ 3.

_____ 4.

_____ 5.

_____ 6.

_____ 7.

_____ 8.

_____ 9.

(Continued on next page)

53

_____ 10. To bore holes ¼″ to 1″ in diameter, use a(n) ____ ____ .

_____ 11. To bore holes for making dowel joints, use a(n) ____ ____ .

_____ 12. To bore holes larger than one inch, use a(n) ____ ____ .

_____ 13. A ____ is used to hold and operate bits when boring by hand.

_____ 14. To bore a shallow hole with a flat bottom, use a(n)
      A. bit stock drill.
      B. auger bit.
      C. depth gauge.
      D. Foerstner bit.
      E. hand drill.

_____ 15. To limit how deep you drill or bore a hole, use a(n) ____ ____ .

_____ 16. To enlarge an existing hole, use
      A. an expansion bit.
      B. a Foerstner bit.
      C. a bit stock drill.
      D. an auger bit.
      E. none of the above

_____ 17. To bore a hole in end grain, use
      A. a Foerstner bit.
      B. a twist drill.
      C. an auger bit.
      D. a hand drill.
      E. none of the above

_____ 18. A bit stock drill is used to
      A. drill a hole in thin stock.
      B. drill a deep hole.
      C. drill small holes for nails and screws.
      D. drill a hole in edge grain.

_____ 19. A tool with a 3-jaw chuck used to hold twist drills is a ____ ____ .

Date _____   **Name** _____

Score: (19 possible) _____

Unit 23
METALWORKING TOOLS

(Text pages 235-237)

Identify the tools in the illustrations.

_____ 1.

_____ 2.

_____ 3.

_____ 4.

_____ 5.

_____ 6.

_____ 7.

_____ 8.

_____ 9.

_____ 10.

_____ 11.

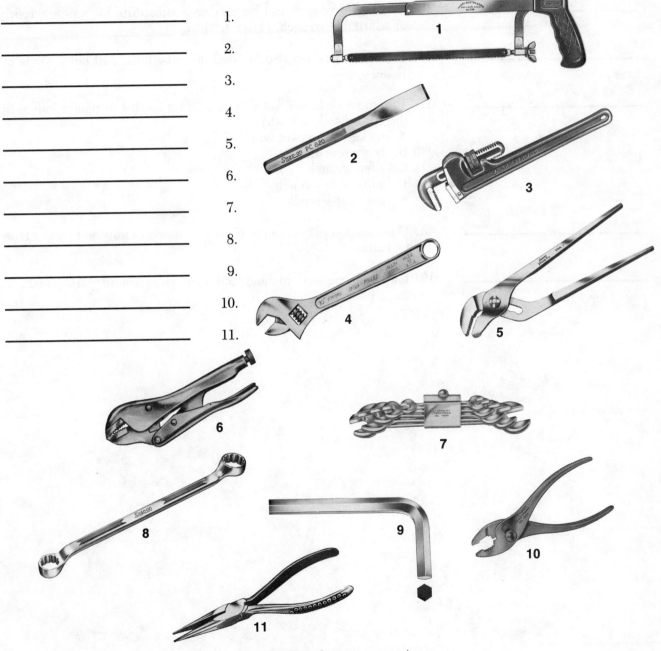

(Continued on next page)

55

_____ 12. What tool is used to cut off a rivet or a nail?

_____ 13. The adjustable wrench develops greatest strength when hand pressure is applied to the side that has the adjustable jaw. (True or False)

_____ 14. To make adjustments where there is limited space for movement, use a(n)
  A. open-end wrench.
  B. vise-grip wrench.
  C. adjustable wrench.
  D. box wrench.
  E. long, flat-nose pliers.

_____ 15. A vise-grip wrench can be used as a substitute for a pipe wrench or adjustable wrench. (True or False)

_____ 16. Pipe wrenches can also be used on rods, nuts, and bolts. (True or False)

_____ 17. To tighten or loosen set screws holding jointer or planer knives in the cutterhead, use a(n)
  A. socket and socket wrench.
  B. box wrench.
  C. allen wrench.
  D. adjustable wrench.
  E. crescent wrench.

_____ 18. Combination pliers are often used on heads of nuts and bolts. (True or False)

_____ 19. Large pliers used to hold and turn large round parts are _____ _____ pliers.

Unit 24
TOOL AND MACHINE MAINTENANCE

(Text pages 237-259)

_____ 1. Hand saw, circular-saw, and band saw blades should be sharpened regularly in the shop. (True or False)

_____ 2. _____ means sharpening the tip of a tool's cutting edge.

_____ 3. _____ means reshaping the cutting edge.

_____ 4. Knives and high-carbon tools should be sharpened with _____ wheels.

_____ 5. Wheels for sharpening tool steel should be made of _____ .

_____ 6. Carbide-tipped tools should be sharpened with a _____ _____ wheel.

_____ 7. A 36-grit grinding wheel has a _____ abrasive texture.

_____ 8. A 120-grit grinding wheel has a _____ abrasive texture.

_____ 9. What is the best tool for cleaning a grinding wheel?

_____ 10. In many sharpening and honing operations, a _____ _____ is needed for faster work, a finer edge, and to keep the stone free of chips.

_____ 11. If a cutting tool is allowed to become too hot during grinding, it will lose its hardness. (True or False)

_____ 12. The correct angle for honing the cutting edge of a plane iron blade is 20 to 25 degrees. (True or False)

_____ 13. The plane-iron blade should have a slight bevel on the back side. (True or False)

_____ 14. When a major bevel is ground with a slight curve, then a secondary bevel is ground to produce the actual cutting edge, the tool is said to be _____ .

_____ 15. When sharpening auger bits, you should file only the outside spurs. (True or False)

(Continued on next page)

_____   16. A screwdriver should be ground so that the sides and edges are tapered and the end is _____ .

_____   17. The bevels on woodturning tools used for cutting should be _____ .

_____   18. Bringing all the teeth of the saw to the same height is known as _____ .

_____   19. The teeth of the hand saw must be reset every time they are sharpened. (True or False)

_____   20. The teeth of crosscut saws are like _____ .

_____   21. The teeth of rip saws are like _____ .

_____   22. The cut the saw makes in the wood is called the _____ .

_____   23. The low parts between the saw teeth are the _____ .

_____   24. Springing over the upper part of each tooth of a saw, alternating left to right, is called _____ the teeth.

_____   25. What is the maximum depth for the procedure in question 24?

_____   26. Carbide-tipped tools need grinding less frequently. (True or False)

_____   27. There is always one more point per inch on a saw blade than there are teeth. (True or False)

_____   28. Use a _____ file for sharpening hand saws and band-saw blades.

_____   29. When filing circular-saw blades, the bevel should be _____ the length of the teeth.

_____   30. Planer knives do not need to be removed from the cutterhead for grinding. (True or False)

_____   31. The bevel ground on planer knives must be straight. (True or False)

_____   32. The best method of setting all the jointer knives at the same height when replacing them is to use a(n) _____ as a straightedge.

_____   33. When sharpening router bits, most grinding and honing should be done on the _____ of the tool.

_____   34. A twist drill should have a point angle of _____ degrees on each side of the axis.

Unit 25
PLANER OR SURFACER

(Text pages 260-266)

_____ 1. The purpose of a planer is to
    A. produce a true surface.
    B. correct twist.
    C. remove wind.
    D. cut stock to uniform thickness.

_____ 2. The ____ planer cuts both the top and bottom of a board at the same time.

_____ 3. The size of a planer is determined by
    A. the thickness of stock it will surface.
    B. the size of the chip breaker.
    C. the width of stock it will surface.
    D. the length of the infeed rolls.

Identify the parts of a two-roll planer head.

_____ 4.

_____ 5.

_____ 6.

_____ 7.

_____ 8.

_____ 9.

_____ 10.

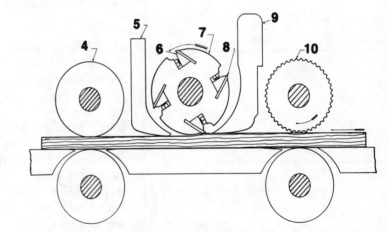

11. A sectional infeed roll allows several pieces of slightly different ____ to be fed into the planer at one time.

12. The ____ ____ keeps the stock firmly pressed to the bed and prevents torn grain.

13. The ____ ____ moves the bed up and down to control the depth of the cut.

(Continued on next page)

_____ 14. Which of the following is *not* considered when determining the feed rate?
    A. the width of stock
    B. the thickness of stock
    C. the kind of wood
    D. the desired surface quality

_____ 15. Before planing a warped board, true one face on the _____ .

_____ 16. Feed stock into the machine with the grain whenever possible. (True or False)

_____ 17. How much stock should the planer remove in one cut?

_____ 18. You should stand directly behind the stock as it is fed into the planer. (True or False)

_____ 19. When removing a large amount of stock, all cuts should be made from one side. (True or False)

_____ 20. When stock has been glued up to make a larger surface, it is impossible to true it on the planer. (True or False)

_____ 21. You should use a(n) _____ _____ when planing thin stock.

_____ 22. Only new, unused lumber should be surfaced. (True or False)

_____ 23. The shortest board that should be run through the machine should be _____ longer than the distance between the infeed and outfeed rolls.

_____ 24. Which of the following is *not* usually a cause of stock sticking or hesitating in the machine?
    A. knives too dull
    B. pressure bar set too low
    C. cut too heavy
    D. upper bars not set low enough

_____ 25. Which of the following is *not* usually a cause of a washboard finish?
    A. knives too dull
    B. feed too slow
    C. joint too heavy
    D. machine not level

Unit 26
CIRCULAR OR VARIETY SAW

(Text pages 267-306)

_____ 1. The ____ holds the saw and revolves.

_____ 2. For all ripping operations, a ____ ____ must be used to guide the work.

_____ 3. For all crosscutting operations, the ____ ____ is used to guide the work.

_____ 4. To control the length of crosscut, clamp a ____ ____ to the type of guide indicated in question 3.

_____ 5. The blade should project about ½″ above the stock. (True or False)

_____ 6. Whenever possible, a(n) ____ should cover the saw to act as a protective device.

_____ 7. A(n) ____ is a piece of metal directly behind the blade that keeps the saw kerf open.

Identify the different types of blades.

_____ 8.

_____ 9.

_____ 10.

_____ 11.

_____ 12. The commercial ____ is an accessory for the circular saw that provides a safe means of cutting end grain.

(Continued on next page)

_____   13. The _____ blade is for general ripping, crosscutting, and mitering.

_____   14. _____ blades are best for cutting hardboard and plastic laminates.

_____   15. One good method of cutting several pieces to the same length is to use the fence as a stop block. (True or False)

_____   16. A _____ across grain is made by tilting the blade to the correct angle and using the miter gage set at right angles.

_____   17. When cutting plywood on the circular saw, always place the stock with the _____ side up.

_____   18. If no helper is available when ripping long stock, use a _____ _____ .

_____   19. A piece of wood that has a notch at the end and is used to move narrow stock as it is being ripped is a(n) _____ _____ or block.

_____   20. A somewhat flexible _____ _____ is used to apply side pressure, pushing the stock gently against the fence, for ripping.

_____   21. When the rip cut is less than 2″, use a _____ _____ to move the stock.

_____   22. Ripping a board to make one or more thinner pieces is called _____ .

_____   23. To cut corner blocks, you should make a _____ _____ .

_____   24. The typical _____ _____ consists of two outside cutters and several inside chippers.

_____   25. A(n) _____ is a slot cut with the grain of the wood.

_____   26. A(n) _____ is a slot cut across the grain of the wood.

_____   27. Joint cuts are made with a combination blade or a(n) _____ _____ .

_____   28. When cutting a corner dado, a _____ _____ is needed to hold the stock against the miter gage.

_____   29. In cutting a dovetail dado, the blade must be set at an angle of _____ degrees.

_____   30. Enclosed mortises can be cut with a dado head on the circular saw. (True or False)

_____   31. A(n) _____ is a rounded groove that can be made by feeding stock across the saw at a slight angle.

_____   32. When making saw-cut moldings, the kerf should be _____ the thickness of the stock.

_____   33. Most moldings are cut on the edge of stock. (True or False)

Unit 27
RADIAL-ARM SAW

(Text pages 306-336)

_____ 1. The radial-arm saw is better for ripping than the circular saw. (True or False)

_____ 2. For crosscutting, the ____ is held in a fixed position.

_____ 3. For ripping, the ____ is held in a fixed position.

_____ 4. The tracks of the radial-arm saw should be lubricated often. (True or False)

_____ 5. When replacing the blade, the teeth should point in the direction of rotation. (True or False)

Identify the numbered items in the illustration.

_____ 6.

_____ 7.

_____ 8.

_____ 9.

_____ 10.

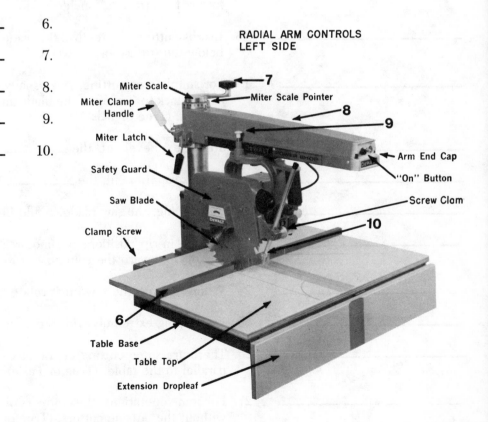

RADIAL ARM CONTROLS
LEFT SIDE

Miter Scale
Miter Clamp Handle
Miter Latch
Safety Guard
Saw Blade
Clamp Screw
Miter Scale Pointer
Arm End Cap
"On" Button
Screw Clamp
Table Base
Table Top
Extension Dropleaf

(Continued on next page)

63

Identify the numbered items in the illustration.

_____ 11.

_____ 12.

_____ 13.

_____ 14.

_____ 15.

_____ 16.

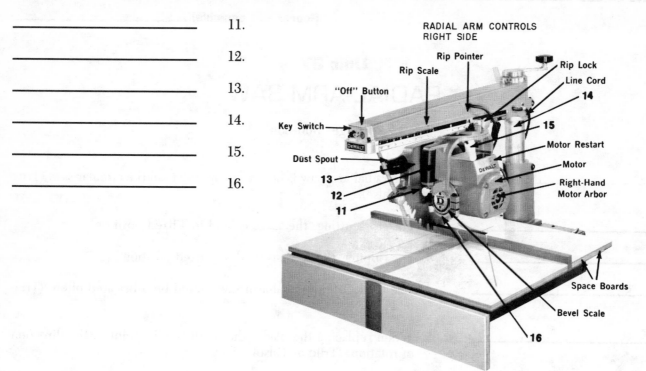

RADIAL ARM CONTROLS
RIGHT SIDE

Rip Pointer

Rip Scale

Rip Lock

Line Cord

"Off" Button

14

Key Switch

15

Motor Restart

Dust Spout

Motor

13

Right-Hand
Motor Arbor

12

11

Space Boards

Bevel Scale

16

_____ 17. On most machines each full turn of the elevating handle raises or lowers the arm _____ inch(es).

_____ 18. In crosscutting, the teeth of the blade should be about _____ inch(es) below the surface of the wood.

_____ 19. For simple crosscutting, it is usually easier to keep the longer part of the stock to the left of the blade and use your right hand to guide the saw. (True or False)

_____ 20. To make a bevel cut, the _____ _____ is tilted to the correct angle.

_____ 21. To make a miter cut, the _____ _____ is rotated to the correct angle.

_____ 22. For ripping, the saw blade should be _____ to the fence.

_____ 23. For the in-rip position, the motor is toward the outside, and the saw blade toward the column. (True or False)

_____ 24. When ripping, the saw must rotate toward you. (True or False)

_____ 25. For ripping extremely wide stock, use the _____ position.

_____ 26. There are some cutting operations in which the blade is actually parallel to the table. (True or False)

_____ 27. For some operations, the chippers of the dado head are used alone, without the outside cutters. (True or False)

(Continued on next page)

64

_____

28. A blind dado can be made by using a(n) ___ ___ on the arm to control the distance the saw will move.

_____

29. When using the dado head for ploughing, you should feed the stock into the rotation of the blade. (True or False)

_____

30. It is possible to do both cutting and dadoing at the same time by combining a dado head and a blade. (True or False)

_____

31. For molding operations it is necessary to install a different fence than for sawing. (True or False)

Unit 28
BAND SAW

(Text pages 337-351)

_____

1. The thickness of stock that can be cut on the band saw depends on the distance between the table top and the ____ ____ in its top position.

_____

2. The ____ ____ gives the upper wheel a little play.

_____

3. The ____ ____ moves the upper wheel forward or back.

Identify the controls in the illustration.

_____ 4.

_____ 5.

_____ 6.

_____ 7.

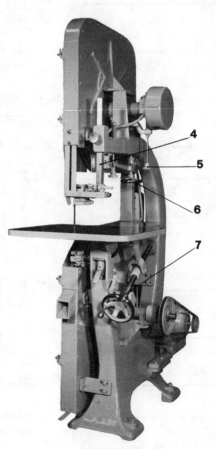

_____

8. The blade is held in place by two pairs of ____ ____ , one above and one below the table.

_____

9. To adjust for cutting wood of different thicknesses, the ____ ____ is raised or lowered.

_____

10. Use a ____ blade for cutting sharp curves.

(Continued on next page)

_____ 11. The blade is made to track on the center of the wheel by:
          A. tilting the upper wheel.
          B. tilting the table.
          C. tilting the lower wheel.
          D. adjusting the guide blocks.

_____ 12. Blades should always "give" slightly when pressed. (True or False)

_____ 13. The clearance between the blade and the guide pins should be approximately the thickness of ____ ____ ____ .

_____ 14. You should cut directly on the layout lines. (True or False)

_____ 15. The upper blade guide should be adjusted to clear the stock by about ____ .

_____ 16. Long cuts should be made before short ones. (True or False)

_____ 17. Use a mortising chisel or a(n) ____ ____ to make starting or turning holes in the waste stock.

_____ 18. On short or complicated curves, first make several ____ cuts almost to the layout line.

_____ 19. When cutting hardwood or wood that has a lot of pitch, apply ____ to the blade to help the cutting.

_____ 20. If a blade tends to run to one side, it is said to be ____ .

_____ 21. Which of the following would *not* be a cause of the blade tending to run to one side?
          A. guide too loose
          B. blade too wide
          C. more set on one side of teeth than the other
          D. slight wear on one side of blade

_____ 22. The band saw is better for most resawing jobs than the circular saw. (True or False)

_____ 23. You can rip freehand by using the thumb of your left hand as a guide. (True or False)

_____ 24. The best method of resawing is to use a(n) ____ ____ as a guide.

_____ 25. Cutting decorative shapes from two adjoining surfaces of a square or rectangular piece of stock is called ____ ____ .

_____ 26. The simplest method of cutting a single circular piece is to do it freehand. (True or False)

_____ 27. Using a wood pattern as a guide is an accurate method of cutting all kinds of duplicate parts. (True or False)

_____ 28. One method of cutting duplicate parts is to first cut thicker stock to shape, then ____ it to get thinner pieces of the desired shape.

Unit 29
SCROLL SAW

(Text pages 351-359)

_____   1. The scroll saw has little use in furniture production. (True or False)

Identify the numbered parts in the illustration.

_____   2.

_____   3.

_____   4.

_____   5.

_____   6.

_____   7.

_____   8.

_____   9.

_____   10.

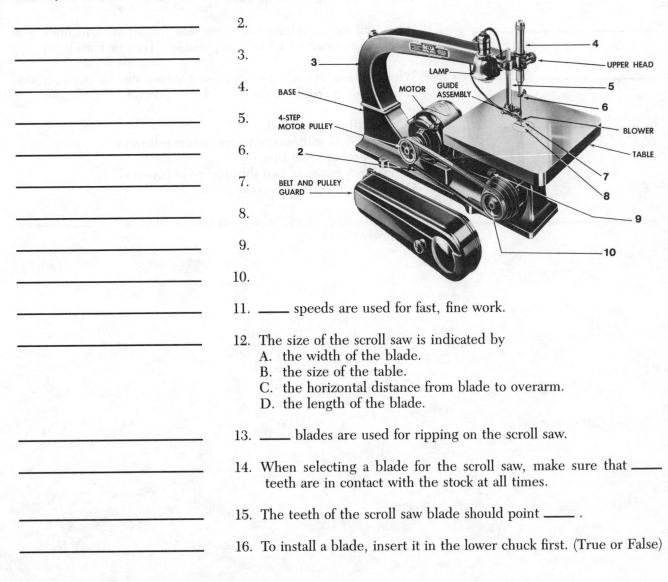

_____   11. _____ speeds are used for fast, fine work.

_____   12. The size of the scroll saw is indicated by
                                 A. the width of the blade.
                                 B. the size of the table.
                                 C. the horizontal distance from blade to overarm.
                                 D. the length of the blade.

_____   13. _____ blades are used for ripping on the scroll saw.

_____   14. When selecting a blade for the scroll saw, make sure that _____
                                 teeth are in contact with the stock at all times.

_____   15. The teeth of the scroll saw blade should point _____ .

_____   16. To install a blade, insert it in the lower chuck first. (True or False)

(Continued on next page)

_____ 17. Most scroll saws have a universal ___ ___ which can be easily turned to accommodate blades of varying thickness.

_____ 18. The work is held against the table by the ___ .

_____ 19. ___ blades have a sharpened upper end and are fastened only in the lower chuck.

_____ 20. Parts cut with the scroll saw need very little or no sanding. (True or False)

_____ 21. For external cutting, much of the waste stock should be removed with the ___ ___ .

_____ 22. Always feed the stock straight against the teeth, even when turning a shallow corner. (True or False)

_____ 23. When cutting an internal opening that has all straight lines, you should use as narrow a blade as possible. (True or False)

_____ 24. When cutting a bevel, the work must always stay on the same side of the blade. (True or False)

_____ 25. When cutting thin metal,
A. rub it well with waxed paper to lubricate it.
B. use a saber saw blade.
C. clamp it between two thin pieces of plywood.
D. you must use a high speed.

_____ 26. To finish metal edges, small files can be held in the ___ ___ of the lower chuck.

Unit 30
PORTABLE SAWS AND PLANES

(Text pages 360-369)

_____ 1. The portable power saw can be used to trim boards after they have been nailed in place. (True or False)

_____ 2. The portable power saw cuts from the top down. (True or False)

_____ 3. When using the portable power saw for cutting plywood, always cut with the good surface facing ____ .

_____ 4. The top surface of the cut made by the portable power saw is smoother than the bottom surface. (True or False)

_____ 5. For safety, the portable power saw blade should clear the bottom of the work by about ____ inch(es).

_____ 6. To cut a bevel with the portable power saw, the ____ must be tilted to the correct angle.

_____ 7. When cutting a bevel with the electric hand saw, the long side of the bevel should be at the bottom of the cut. (True or False)

_____ 8. When using the portable power saw, a miter cut can be made freehand or with a ____ ____ .

_____ 9. To make a really accurate cut when ripping with the portable power saw, use a(n) ____ ____ .

_____ 10. A(n) ____ cut is an internal opening cut in the middle of a wide board with the portable power saw while holding the saw guard out of the way.

_____ 11. When using extension cords up to 100′ in length with portable saws, the wire must be at least ____ gage.

_____ 12. A ____ ____ saw is a power saw mounted in a miter box and is very useful for fitting and installing moldings.

_____ 13. A ____ saw is a portable power saw mounted in a large rack and used for cutting plywood, hardboard, and other sheet materials.

_____ 14. The ____ saw is a portable saw which operates much like a scroll saw and is for cutting internal and external curves.

(Continued on next page)

15. The blade for the saw in question 14 is installed with the cutting edges pointing ＿＿ .

16. For fastest cutting in ⅜″ or thicker material, saber saw blades should have a ＿＿ tooth design.

17. Cutting an inside cut with a hand jig saw without drilling a clearance hole is called ＿＿ cutting.

18. A true circle can be cut with the bayonet saw by using the ＿＿ ＿＿ .

19. A ＿＿ saw is basically a power hack saw or keyhole saw that is held like a drill.

20. For cutting plastic laminates with the saw in question 19, use ＿＿ speed.

21. This saw has a multi-position ＿＿ that can be adjusted for depth and angle of cut.

22. Which blade would be best for making rough cuts in softwood with the saw in question 19?
    A. 10
    B. 8
    C. 5½
    D. 3½
    E. none of the above

23. When planing edges of plywood with the electric hand plane, you should
    A. use a very slow speed all along the cut.
    B. clamp a piece of scrap wood at the end of the plywood.
    C. make only very shallow cuts.
    D. use the same speed and pressure as for soft woods.

24. Both hands must be used when operating the power block plane. (True or False)

Unit 31
JOINTER

(Text pages 370-380)

_____ 1. Which of the following does *not* affect the smoothness of the cut?
- A. number of knives
- B. the feed
- C. the speed of rotation
- D. type of wood being surfaced

_____ 2. Only the edges of S2S lumber need to be surfaced. (True or False)

_____ 3. Remove warp from rough lumber by
- A. planing both surfaces on the planer.
- B. surfacing all four sides.
- C. cutting one face flat on the jointer.
- D. none of the above

Identify the numbered parts of a jointer.

_____ 4.

_____ 5.

_____ 6.

_____ 7.

_____ 8.

_____ 9.

_____ 10.

_____ 11.

_____ 12.

_____ 13.

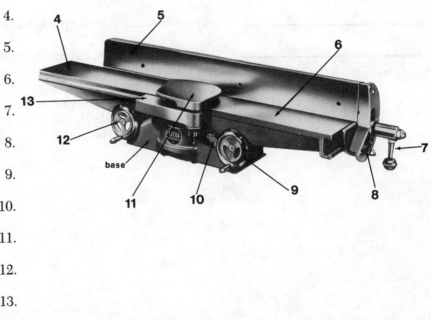

14. Before you begin cutting, make sure the _____ table is exactly the same height as the knives at their highest point.

(Continued on next page)

15. If the table is too high, it will cut a _____ .

16. If the table is too low, it will cut a _____ .

17. A(n) _____ is a small concave cut at the end of the stock.

18. The depth of cut is determined by the adjustment of the _____ _____ .

19. Never make a cut deeper than _____ .

20. Only _____ inch should be removed for a finish cut.

21. The _____ is tilted to make bevel or chamfer cuts.

22. Always stand at the _____ of the front table.

23. When a board placed on a flat surface rocks back and forth on the diagonal corners, it has _____ .

24. A board is _____ if the edges are concave on one side and convex on the other.

25. To surface a board that is cupped, place the convex side down. (True or False)

26. When edge jointing, the best surface of the stock should be placed against the fence. (True or False)

27. A(n) _____ is a sharp edge cut at a slight bevel.

28. A taper can be cut on the jointer by
    A. setting the fence at an angle.
    B. raising the rear table.
    C. lowering the front table.
    D. lowering both the front and rear tables.
    E. none of the above.

Unit 32
SHAPER

(Text pages 381-393)

_____ 1. The shaper is a relatively safe machine to use. (True or False)

_____ 2. The shaper will cut different thicknesses of stock by moving the ____ up or down.

_____ 3. ____ ____ are used to hold the work firmly against the fence and table.

_____ 4. The ____ can be used for vertical shaping operations.

Match the cutters on the left with the descriptions on the right.

_____ 5. three-lip cutters

_____ 6. grooving saws

_____ 7. three-knife safety cutter-head

A. can be used for making many types of joints
B. can use same molding knives as for circular or radial-arm saw
C. considered the safest

_____ 8. Always feed the work into the cutters in the direction opposite to cutter rotation. (True or False)

_____ 9. The shortest piece that can be safely shaped without a jig is ____ .

_____ 10. Stock must be at least ____ wide when shaping end grain.

_____ 11. Keep your hands at least ____ inch(es) away from the cutter at all times.

_____ 12. Cutters should be installed with the ____ ____ towards the table.

_____ 13. Whenever possible, install the cutter so that the ____ of the stock is being shaped.

_____ 14. For most operations, the ____ controls depth of cut.

_____ 15. When cutting must be done without a fence, ____ ____ must be used.

(Continued on next page)

_____ 16. When shaping is done on irregular shaped material, a(n) _____ _____ must be used.

_____ 17. In the regular method of shaping, the cutter rotates _____ .

_____ 18. In the inverted method of shaping, stock is fed from _____ _____ _____ .

_____ 19. If the complete edge is to be shaped,
    A. both fences must be in line with each other.
    B. a wood fence should be used.
    C. the rear fence must be adjusted to form a support.
    D. the inverted method of shaping should be used.
    E. spring hold-downs and a starting pin should be used.

_____ 20. For face shaping, use a(n) _____ _____ with a spindle hole.

_____ 21. When end grain is to be shaped a(n) _____ _____ or wide board should be used to help support the work.

_____ 22. Depth collars can be used above, below, or between the cutters. (True or False)

_____ 23. When cutting freehand, use depth collars and a(n) _____ _____ .

_____ 24. When using depth collars, only part of the edge can be shaped. (True or False)

_____ 25. The safety-ring spindle guard must clear the thickness of the stock by about
    A. ⅛ inch.
    B. ¼ inch.
    C. ½ inch.
    D. 1 inch.

_____ 26. When shaping freehand, place the starting pin in the right-hand hole if the cutter is rotating _____ .

_____ 27. When shaping with patterns, the workpiece is attached to the pattern and the pattern rides against the _____ .

_____ 28. When shaping on the radial-arm saw, use a two-piece adjustable _____ for most operations.

_____ 29. Shaping can be done on the drill press by replacing the _____ with a shaper adapter.

Unit 33
ROUTERS

(Text pages 394-412)

_____ 1. On a floor router, the work moves; with a portable router, the tool moves. (True or False)

_____ 2. With a _____ router, the base can rest flat on the workpiece and the bit is lowered to the starting position.

_____ 3. A _____ _____ attached to the end of the motor holds the cutting tools.

_____ 4. On the depth adjusting ring, each notch equals _____ _____ _____ .

Identify the router bits in the illustrations.

_____ 5.

_____ 6.

_____ 7.

_____ 8.

_____ 9.

_____ 10.

_____ 11.

_____ 12.

_____ 13.

_____ 14.

_____ 15.

_____ 16.

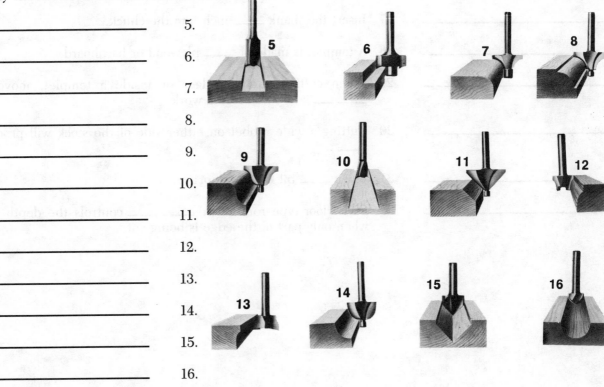

(Continued on next page)

_____   17. Many bits have a ____ ____ which limits the depth of cut by riding along the edge of the work.

Match the bit on the left with the job for which it is commonly used on the right.

_____ 18. chamfer

_____ 19. Roman ogee

_____ 20. straight

_____ 21. "V" grooving

_____ 22. cove

_____ 23. dovetail

_____ 24. veining

_____ 25. rabbet

A. decorative inside edge of paneled doors
B. dropleaf table joint
C. joint for a drawer
D. 45-degree bevel on edges
E. decorative figure routing; raised letters
F. grooves, dadoes, inlay work
G. lip doors
H. imitate plank construction

_____   26. When doing freehand routing to make letters, a(n) ____ bit is usually used.

_____   27. Insert the shank ____ inch into the chuck.

_____   28. A templet is made of ____ plywood or hardboard.

_____   29. When cutting straight edges or inside a templet, move ____ ____ ____ as you face the work.

_____   30. Cutting a wide rabbet on either side of the stock will produce a ____ .

_____   31. Use a ____ bit to cut a mortise.

_____   32. On a floor-type router a(n) ____ ____ controls the depth of cut when only part of the edge is being cut.

Unit 34
DRILLING AND BORING MACHINES

(Text pages 412-433)

_____ 1. ____ refers to cutting holes that are larger than $\frac{1}{4}''$.

_____ 2. ____ refers to cutting holes that are $\frac{1}{4}''$ or smaller.

_____ 3. ____ boring is necessary when installing dowels.

_____ 4. ____ drilling is done when installing screws.

_____ 5. Dowels have largely replaced the mortise-and-tenon joint in cabinet and furniture making. (True or False)

_____ 6. The size of the drill press is determined by
A. the depth of hole that can be cut on it.
B. the size of the chuck.
C. the length of the quill.
D. the distance from the drill to the column.

_____ 7. Generally, a(n) ____ ____ is used to hold the cutting tool on the drill press.

_____ 8. For shaping, routing, and planing on the drill press, use ____ speeds.

_____ 9. The ____ ____ ____ has a drill head that can be moved and tilted.

Match the cutting tool with the proper description.

_____ 10. spur machine bit   A. round holes with flat bottoms
                                                B. cuts holes $\frac{5}{8}''$ to $3\frac{1}{2}''$ diameter
_____ 11. multi-spur bit   C. best for dowel holes
                                                D. bore plywood without tearing
_____ 12. hole saw   E. also called spade bit

_____ 13. speed bit

_____ 14. Foerstner bit

_____ 15. A(n) ____ ____ can bore holes at any angle, regardless of grain or knots.

_____ 16. Masonry bits must be used at high speeds. (True or False)

(Continued on next page)

Identify the cutting tools in the illustrations.

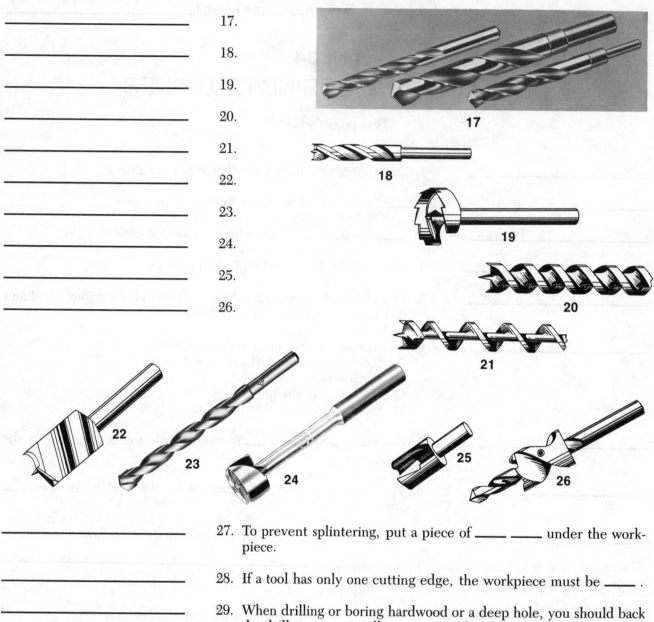

_____ 17.

_____ 18.

_____ 19.

_____ 20.

_____ 21.

_____ 22.

_____ 23.

_____ 24.

_____ 25.

_____ 26.

_____ 27. To prevent splintering, put a piece of ____ ____ under the work-piece.

_____ 28. If a tool has only one cutting edge, the workpiece must be ____ .

_____ 29. When drilling or boring hardwood or a deep hole, you should back the drill out occasionally to remove the chips. (True or False)

_____ 30. The maximum distance the drill will move is called the ____ ____ .

_____ 31. To bore holes in dowel rod or the edge of circular stock, a(n) ____ ____ is needed.

_____ 32. Enlarging part of the outer end of a hole is called ____ .

_____ 33. Dowel holes must be drilled with a ____ clearance at each end.

_____ 34. How thick should dowels be in comparison to the thickness of the stock they are holding?

80

Unit 35
MORTISER AND TENONER

(Text pages 433-441)

_____   1. Extra pressure is needed on the foot level when cutting hardwoods. (True or False)

_____   2. On deep cuts, you should back out often to clean out the hole. (True or False)

Match the lettered parts shown in the illustration to the proper names.

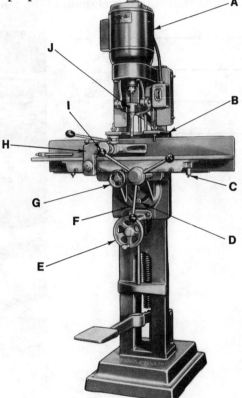

_____   3. stock hold down

_____   4. stock clamp

_____   5. cross feed hand wheel

_____   6. hand wheel for stroke adjustment

_____   7. table tilt lock

_____   8. table angle gage

_____   9. stop for longitudinal level

_____   10. longitudinal travel hand wheel

_____   11. table hand wheel for vertical adjustment

_____   12. set screw for hollow chisel

_____   13. The ____ has openings for the chips to come out.

_____   14. The ____ clears away the core of the mortise.

_____   15. The chisel must be slightly longer than the bit so that the bottom of the hole will be squared. (True or False)

(Continued on next page)

_____ 16. Use a(n) ____ ____ to properly align the chisel.

_____ 17. In adjusting a mortising chisel, make sure it touches the table at the bottom of the stroke. (True or False)

_____ 18. When cutting with the mortiser, the cuts should all be consecutive, one right after the other until the full length of the cut is made (True or False)

_____ 19. When cutting a mortise on a cabriole leg, use a(n) ____ ____ to keep the leg in position.

_____ 20. When using a mortising attachment on the drill press, a(n) ____ keeps the work against the fence and table.

_____ 21. If only a few tenons must be cut, it is much faster to use a radial-arm or circular saw than a tenoner. (True or False)

Identify the parts shown in this closeup of the tenoner.

_____ 22.

_____ 23.

_____ 24.

_____ 25.

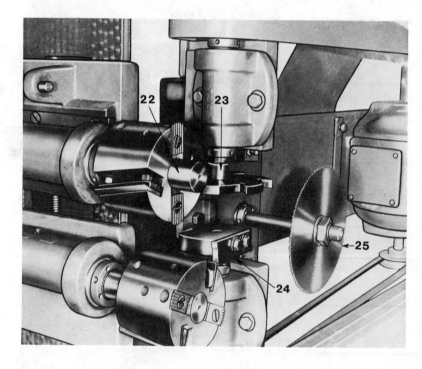

_____ 26. On the single-end tenoner, the stock passes first through the ____ ____ .

Unit 36
SANDING MACHINES AND COATED ABRASIVES

(Text pages 441-460)

_____   1. ____ is a grayish-white or eggshell color abrasive used for hand sanding.

_____   2. ____ ____ is a brown abrasive considered excellent for the harder woods.

_____   3. ____ is a reddish-brown abrasive used primarily for finish sanding.

_____   4. ____ ____ is a greenish-black abrasive used on fibrous woods, plastic, and relatively soft materials.

_____   5. Which abrasive is considered the toughest and most durable?

_____   6. The higher the number, the finer the grit size. (True or False)

_____   7. What do the letters after the grit number designate?

_____   8. Which letter designation would you choose for light hand sanding?
  A. J
  B. A
  C. X
  D. C

_____   9. The electrocoating method of applying abrasive grains is better than the gravity coating method. (True or False)

_____ 10. An abrasive grain coating in which the grains completely cover the adhesive is called ____ coat.

_____ 11. For rough sanding and removing paint and varnish, choose ____ coat abrasives.

_____ 12. For finish sanding, choose ____ coat abrasives.

_____ 13. Controlled breaking of the adhesive bond is called ____ .

_____ 14. The purpose of this controlled bending process is to make the paper ____ .

_____ 15. In ____ the bending of the abrasive sheet is done in all directions.

(Continued on next page)

_____ 16. Hardwoods generally require a slightly coarser grit than softwoods. (True or False)

_____ 17. To save time when sanding, you can go from a coarse grit directly to a fine one. (True or False)

_____ 18. What type grit should be used to remove the final rough texture before finish sanding?

_____ 19. For surface sanding, the belt sander should be in the ____ position.

_____ 20. For sanding end grain, put the belt sander in the ____ position.

_____ 21. Disk sanders should not be used for surface sanding in cabinet-making. (True or False)

_____ 22. The ____ sander is designed primarily for use on edges and irregular curves.

_____ 23. Lower the portable belt sander in such a way that
   A. the front of the sander touches the work first.
   B. the heel of the sander touches the work first.
   C. the belt comes flatly and evenly in contact with the work all at once.
   D. you begin at the very edge of the work.

_____ 24. When using the portable belt sander, cross sanding may sometimes be necessary. (True or False)

Name the type of sanding action shown in each illustration.

_____ 25.

_____ 26.

_____ 27.

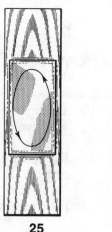 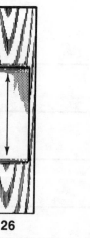 

25   **26**   **27**

_____ 28. Which action on the finishing sander produces the best surface?

_____ 29. Which abrasive is most commonly used for hand sanding in cabinetmaking?

_____ 30. Be sure to thoroughly remove any glue or pencil marks by carefully hand sanding them. (True or False)

Unit 37
WOOD LATHE

(Text pages 461-487)

_____

_____

1. The _____ is permanently mounted on the left end of the lathe.

2. The _____ holds the dead center and can be moved to many positions along the bed.

Identify these turning tools.

_____

_____

_____

_____

_____

3.

4.

5.

6.

7.

8.

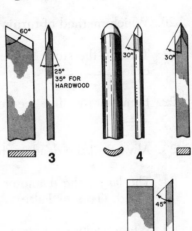

Match the tools on the left with the uses on the right.

_____ 9. flat tools

_____ 10. spear-point tools

_____ 11. round-nose tools

_____ 12. gouges

_____ 13. skews

_____ 14. parting tools

A. for rough cutting stock to round shape
B. for smooth cuts to finish a surface
C. to cut a recess or groove
D. to finish the inside of recesses or corners
E. for scraping a straight surface
F. for scraping concave recesses and circular grooves

_____

_____

15. Always remove the _____ _____ before sanding and polishing.

16. The _____ _____ is needed for checking the outside diameter of turned work.

(Continued on next page)

_____ 17. The _____ _____ is used for laying out distances from the end of stock and locating the center of an irregularly shaped piece.

Identify the method of turning in each illustration.

_____ 18.

_____ 19.

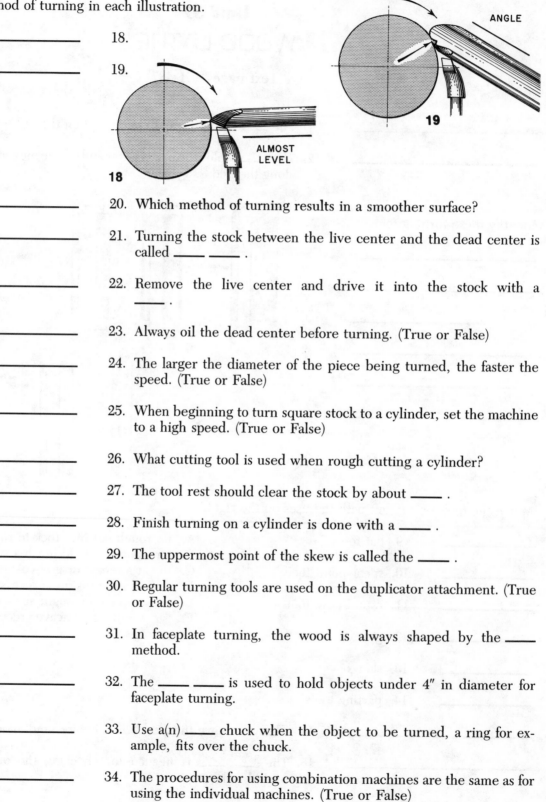

_____ 20. Which method of turning results in a smoother surface?

_____ 21. Turning the stock between the live center and the dead center is called _____ _____ .

_____ 22. Remove the live center and drive it into the stock with a _____ .

_____ 23. Always oil the dead center before turning. (True or False)

_____ 24. The larger the diameter of the piece being turned, the faster the speed. (True or False)

_____ 25. When beginning to turn square stock to a cylinder, set the machine to a high speed. (True or False)

_____ 26. What cutting tool is used when rough cutting a cylinder?

_____ 27. The tool rest should clear the stock by about _____ .

_____ 28. Finish turning on a cylinder is done with a _____ .

_____ 29. The uppermost point of the skew is called the _____ .

_____ 30. Regular turning tools are used on the duplicator attachment. (True or False)

_____ 31. In faceplate turning, the wood is always shaped by the _____ method.

_____ 32. The _____ _____ is used to hold objects under 4" in diameter for faceplate turning.

_____ 33. Use a(n) _____ chuck when the object to be turned, a ring for example, fits over the chuck.

_____ 34. The procedures for using combination machines are the same as for using the individual machines. (True or False)

Unit 38
BASIC CONSTRUCTION PROBLEMS

(Text pages 489-507)

_____   1. Which of the three methods of making a large surface has the most problems with warpage?

_____   2. What does the furniture industry use for large surfaces?

_____   3. In building construction, what are large surfaces of cabinets and built-ins made from?

_____   4. When gluing up pieces of solid stock, the growth rings should run in the same direction. (True or False)

_____   5. Wood changes in size more across the grain than with the grain. (True or False)

_____   6. In best-quality construction, edge banding is attached to plywood edges with a(n) ___ ___ .

_____   7. Only ___ -dried lumber should be used for cabinetmaking.

_____   8. Lumber for furniture should have less than ___ per cent moisture content.

_____   9. When wood reaches a balance with the air at a certain temperature and humidity, the amount of moisture it contains is called the ___ ___ content.

_____   10. Cold air can hold more moisture than warm air. (True or False)

_____   11. Humidity control is needed both summer and winter. (True or False)

_____   12. When using a moisture meter, it is best to test the ___ ___ .

_____   13. ___ is a chemical treatment to give wood a high degree of dimensional stability.

_____   14. The chemical treatment in question 13 should only be done to freshly cut, green wood. (True or False)

_____   15. Woods with higher specific gravity machine better than lighter woods. (True or False)

_____   16. The higher the specific gravity, the harder the wood. (True or False)

(Continued on next page)

_____ 17. Fast-growing species of wood have more growth rings per inch and are therefore easier to machine. (True or False)

_____ 18. _____ grain is a cross grain problem caused by sawing a board in a particular way.

_____ 19. _____ grain is caused by fibers of the tree growing around the trunk rather than vertically.

_____ 20. _____ grain is caused by fiber ends that slope in opposite directions.

_____ 21. The cross grain that can cause the most problems with warpage and machining is _____ grain.

_____ 22. Flat-grained lumber shrinks much more than quarter-sawed. (True or False)

_____ 23. The denser the wood, the more it tends to shrink. (True or False)

_____ 24. As a rule, how many knife marks per inch should there be on machine-planed dry lumber?

Match the planing and surfacing defects in the left column with the proper description.

_____ 25. machine burns

_____ 26. chipped grain

_____ 27. raised grain

_____ 28. fuzzy grain

_____ 29. chip marks

A. small particles broken off below line of cut
B. shallow dents
C. fibers not cut cleanly
D. black marks across the wood
E. rough spot where annual ring is above the surface

_____ 30. Harder woods sand better than softer ones. (True or False)

_____ 31. To assure compatibility of color and grain, you should surface at least three times as much lumber as needed for a particular product. (True or False)

Identify the type of construction on each of these drawers.

_____ 32.

_____ 33.

_____ 34.

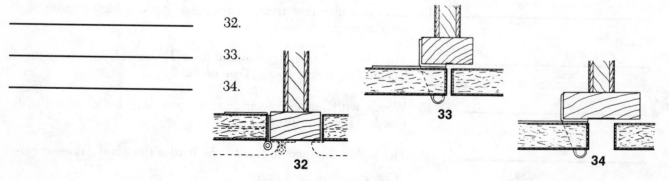

Unit 39
CABINETMAKING JOINTS

(Text pages 507-533)

_____ 1. Any joint that is good for holding solid wood parts is also good for holding plywood. (True or False)

_____ 2. Using dowels with a butt joint makes just as strong a joint as a mortise and tenon. (True or False)

_____ 3. The _____ method of laying out a joint involves placing one piece over another to do the marking.

_____ 4. Quality joints are always glued under pressure. (True or False)

_____ 5. The moisture content of dowels should be _____ per cent or less.

_____ 6. When using dowels, always use two or more. (True or False)

_____ 7. What should the diameter of a dowel be in comparison to the thickness of the wood?

Match the joint strengtheners on the left with their proper description.

_____ 8. dowel

_____ 9. plate

_____ 10. spline

_____ 11. key

_____ 12. glue block

_____ 13. corner block

A. sometimes called a feather
B. thin piece of material inserted in a groove between two pieces of wood
C. small triangular or rectangular piece of wood fastened to two adjoining surfaces
D. triangular piece of wood used to brace frames or leg and rail joints
E. pin or peg that fits into two matching holes
F. flat, football-shaped piece that fits in grooves cut in pieces to be joined

_____ 14. If using a spline to join solid wood, the spline should also be of solid wood. (True or False)

_____ 15. In the _____ joint, the square end of one piece fits against the flat surface or edge of another piece.

_____ 16. _____ joints are made with the grain of the two parts running parallel, but the growth rings facing opposite directions.

(Continued on next page)

_____

_____

_____

_____

_____

_____

_____

17. The ____ joint is made by cutting an L-shaped groove across the edge or end of one piece and fitting the other piece into this to form the joint.

18. A simple ____ joint is made by cutting a groove across the edge of one piece and fitting the butt end of the second piece into this groove.

19. ____ joints are made by cutting away half the thickness of both boards so that, when fitted together, the surfaces are flush.

20. The ____ joint is an angle joint that hides the end grain of both pieces.

21. When a joint is needed to provide a supporting ledge, such as for shelves, the ____ joint is a good one to use.

22. For a mortise-and-tenon joint, the tenon should be ____ the thickness of the stock.

23. The ____ joint is found in the finest grades of drawer construction.

Identify the joints in the illustrations.

_____   24.

_____   25.

_____   26.

_____   27.

_____   28.

_____   29.

_____   30.

_____   31.

_____   32.

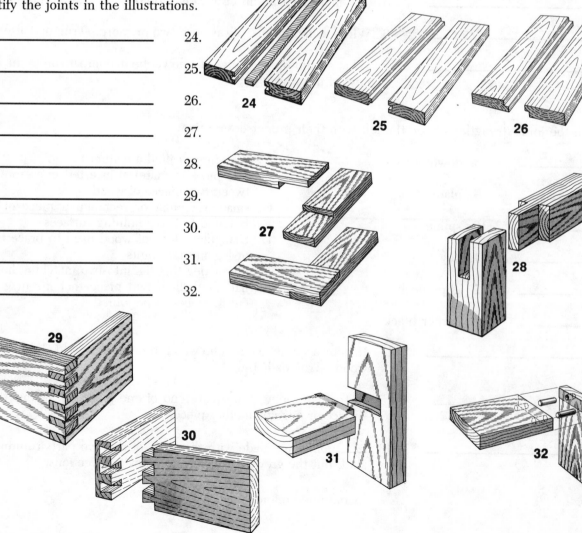

24

25

26

27

28

29

30

31

32

Unit 40
GLUING AND CLAMPING

(Text pages 533-551)

_____ 1. Edge-to-edge gluing is easier to do than face-to-face. (True or False)

_____ 2. Extra glue is needed for fastening end grain. (True or False)

_____ 3. The amount of moisture in the wood may affect the rate at which glue dries, but has little effect on the strength of the finished joint. (True or False)

_____ 4. All pieces that are glued should be clamped. (True or False)

Match the kinds of adhesives on the left with their proper description.

_____ 5. plastic resin glue

_____ 6. casein

_____ 7. resorcinol

_____ 8. contact cement

_____ 9. epoxy resin

_____ 10. urea resin

_____ 11. aliphatic resin

_____ 12. polyvinyl or white liquid glue

_____ 13. animal glue

A. best for exterior use; completely waterproof
B. colorless glue line; quick-setting
C. two-part adhesive; good for gap-filling
D. first choice for furniture; one of best gap-filling
E. best for electronic gluing equipment
F. adheres immediately
G. cream-colored; very high-strength bond; lacks water-resistance
H. powdered; used for furniture veneering; water-resistant
I. good for oily woods; bonds at any temperature above freezing

_____ 14. The best holding devices for wood are ____ ____ .

_____ 15. Protective wood strips placed between clamps and the wood being glued are called ____ .

_____ 16. Hand screws are used only when gluing stock face to face. (True or False)

_____ 17. Holding devices in which one end is adjusted by a friction clutch while the other has a screw for pressure are the ____ ____ .

(Continued on next page)

18. _____ _____ operate like overgrown clothespins.

19. A clamp that can be adjusted instantly by sliding the head along the bar is the _____ clamp.

20. The best clamp to use for round or irregular-shaped pieces is the _____ clamp.

21. The best clamp for assembling frames is the _____ clamp.

22. The moisture content of wood pieces to be glued should be less than _____ per cent.

23. A _____ joint results when boards are surfaced before the moisture content of the glue line equals that of the rest of the wood.

24. In edge gluing, the grain of all pieces should run in the same direction. (True or False)

25. In edge gluing, try to arrange the pieces so growth rings run in the same direction. (True or False)

26. What is the widest that pieces glued edge to edge should be?

27. Using too little glue or too much pressure can result in a(n) _____ _____ .

28. When correct pressure is applied, no glue will be visible at the glue line. (True or False)

29. Stock glued up electronically can be worked immediately after gluing. (True or False)

30. In mortise-and-tenon construction, apply most of the glue to the _____ .

31. After drying, remove excess glue with a(n) _____ _____ .

32. A _____ joint is a weak joint in which the glue became jelly before or immediately after applying pressure.

33. Glue can cause discoloration of some types of wood. (True or False)

Date _____   Name _____

Unit 41
BENDING AND LAMINATING

(Text pages 551-560)

_____ 1. In laminating, the layers must
   A. all be of the same type of wood.
   B. have their grain at right angles to each other.
   C. be glued with waterproof glue.
   D. all have their grain running in the same direction.
   E. have their growth rings going in opposite directions.

_____ 2. Molded plywood is made by the laminating process. (True or False)

_____ 3. Making curved parts by building up layers of small pieces fitted together with the end joints staggered is called the ____ method.

_____ 4. What is the minimum number of layers that should be made in the method in question 3?

_____ 5. Making a board flexible for bending by making a series of deep side-by-side cuts across the board is called ____ ____ .

_____ 6. In the method described in question 5, the saw cuts should be made to within ____ of the outside surface.

_____ 7. A(n) ____ ____ can be made by making equally spaced cuts at an angle across the board.

_____ 8. Which of the following is *not* necessary for bending solid wood to a form?
   A. softening of the wood with moisture
   B. heating the wood
   C. applying pressure to the wood in the form
   D. a wood with low density
   E. All of the above are necessary.

_____ 9. When bending solid wood to a form, the wood must have a moisture content
   A. under 12 per cent.
   B. of at least 30 per cent.
   C. between 12 and 20 percent.
   D. of 25 per cent.

_____ 10. ____ is a term used to describe the process of softening wood with hot water or steam.

(Continued on next page)

_____ 11. What wood has the best bending quality?

_____ 12. When soaking wood for bending, allow ____ ____ for each inch of thickness.

_____ 13. The form or mold for bending can be made of either wood or metal. (True or False)

_____ 14. The bent wood must be thoroughly dry before removing it from the form. (True or False)

_____ 15. When laminating and bending in the school shop, what should the forms be lined with?

_____ 16. The standard thickness of commercial veneer is ____ .

_____ 17. Softwoods are best when making curved laminated pieces. (True or False)

_____ 18. Which of the following adhesives is *not* used for laminating?
A. urea resin
B. casein
C. polyvinyl white glue
D. animal hide glue

_____ 19. When cutting veneer for a curved laminated piece, cut it slightly larger than the desired finished size of the piece. (True or False)

_____ 20. When adjusting the clamps holding the layers being laminated, start at one end, adjust the clamp tightly, and work your way down the piece. (True or False)

Unit 42
VENEERING AND INLAYING

(Text pages 561-575)

Match the veneer-cutting methods on the left with the descriptions on the right.

_____   1. rift cutting

_____   2. flat or plain slicing

_____   3. half-round slicing

_____   4. rotary cutting

_____   5. quarter slicing

A. cut off the log the way a roll of paper would unwind; cut follows growth rings
B. cut perpendicular to the ray cells
C. cut parallel with center of log
D. cut slightly across growth rings by mounting the flitch off center
E. growth rings of the log strike the knives at right angles

_____   6. Veneers cut from two logs of the same species and of very similar color will not look alike if they are cut differently. (True or False)

_____   7. Standard veneers are ____ thick.

_____   8. Veneer imported from many foreign countries is ____ thick.

_____   9. ____ are large, wartlike, deformed growths on the trunk of a tree.

_____   10. ____ are obtained from the stump of a tree.

_____   11. ____ figures have a wavy, rippled pattern.

_____   12. Wood fibers of ____ have a peacock-tail pattern.

_____   13. Wood cut from the ____ have a swirling pattern.

(Continued on next page)

Identify the types of matching.

_____ 14.

_____ 15.

_____ 16.

_____ 17.

_____ 18.

_____ 19.

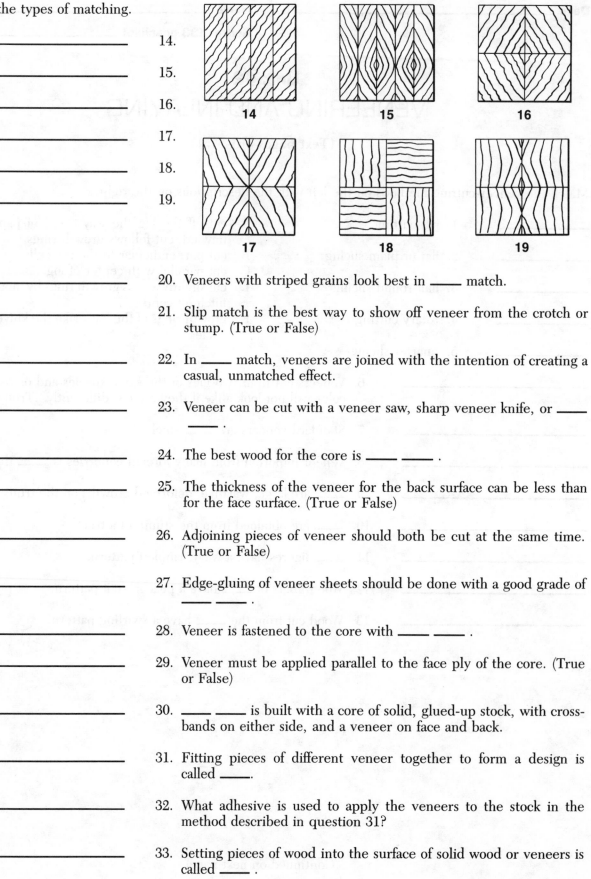

20. Veneers with striped grains look best in _____ match.

_____

21. Slip match is the best way to show off veneer from the crotch or stump. (True or False)

_____

22. In _____ match, veneers are joined with the intention of creating a casual, unmatched effect.

_____

23. Veneer can be cut with a veneer saw, sharp veneer knife, or _____ _____ .

_____

24. The best wood for the core is _____ _____ .

_____

25. The thickness of the veneer for the back surface can be less than for the face surface. (True or False)

_____

26. Adjoining pieces of veneer should both be cut at the same time. (True or False)

_____

27. Edge-gluing of veneer sheets should be done with a good grade of _____ _____ .

_____

28. Veneer is fastened to the core with _____ _____ .

_____

29. Veneer must be applied parallel to the face ply of the core. (True or False)

_____

30. _____ _____ is built with a core of solid, glued-up stock, with cross-bands on either side, and a veneer on face and back.

_____

31. Fitting pieces of different veneer together to form a design is called _____.

_____

32. What adhesive is used to apply the veneers to the stock in the method described in question 31?

_____

33. Setting pieces of wood into the surface of solid wood or veneers is called _____ .

Unit 43
PLASTIC LAMINATES

(Text pages 575-589)

_____   1. The standard thickness of plastic laminate is _____ .

_____   2. _____ grade of plastic laminate is used for kitchen counters, table tops, and desk tops.

_____   3. _____ grade of plastic laminate is designed for heating and forming into short radii for applications around doors and sill ledges.

_____   4. _____ grade is used only for vertical surfaces such as cabinet fronts.

_____   5. All grades of plastic laminate come in the same thickness. (True or False)

_____   6. Backer sheets should be used when a top has an unsupported area of more than _____ square feet.

_____   7. Plastic laminates are relatively inexpensive. (True or False)

_____   8. Plywood used under plastic laminates for horizontal surfaces should be at least _____ thick.

_____   9. Plywood for vertical surfaces should be at least _____ thick.

_____   10. Plastic laminates should not be bonded to particle board. (True or False)

_____   11. Hardboard used under plastic laminates should be the tempered kind. (True or False)

_____   12. The best adhesive to use for on-the-job installation of plastic laminates is _____ _____ .

_____   13. To apply adhesive to a flat surface, use a(n) _____ .

_____   14. Since standard woodworking tools dull rapidly when cutting plastic laminate, _____ cutting tools are recommended.

_____   15. Rough-cut pieces should allow _____ for trimming.

(Continued on next page)

_____ 16. When cutting plastic laminate with the cutoff saw or hand jig saw, the decorative surface should be _____ .

_____ 17. On self edge or edge banding, apply the top surface before applying the edge. (True or False)

Identify the edge treatments illustrated here.

_____ 18.

_____ 19.

_____ 20.

_____ 21.

_____ 22.

_____ 23.

_____ 24.

_____ 25.

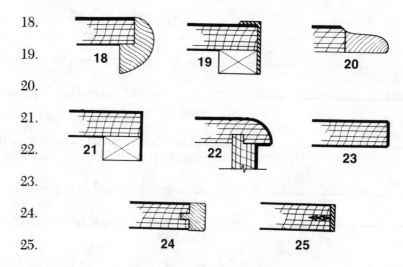

_____ 26. When using contact cement, the surfaces should be adjoined while the adhesive is tacky. (True or False)

_____ 27. Trim edge treatments of plastic laminate with a(n) _____ .

28. What molding requires a saw kerf for installing and is used for table and counter tops?

_____ 29. What molding is used for non-drip edges?

_____ 30. What molding is used for joining a counter top with a backsplash?

Identify the types of molding in the illustrations.

_____ 31.

_____ 32.

_____ 33.

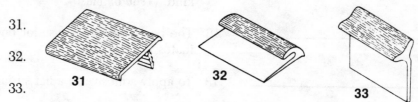

34. When applying plastic laminate to a table top, roll the surface first from one edge to the other, then from one end to the other. (True or False)

Unit 44
FRAME-AND-PANEL CONSTRUCTION

(Text pages 590-602)

_____ 1. Frame-and-panel construction provides a means for a large surface of wood to shrink or swell within a narrow frame. (True or False)

_____ 2. Frame-and-panel construction does not warp, but has only fair dimensional stability. (True or False)

_____ 3. A(n) ___ frame, consisting of two vertical members and two horizontal members, is installed inside cabinets to add stability and serve as drawer supports.

_____ 4. A ___ panel is installed between drawers in better-quality furniture.

Identify the numbered parts of the typical frame.

_____ 5.

_____ 6.

_____ 7.

_____ 8.

_____ 9.

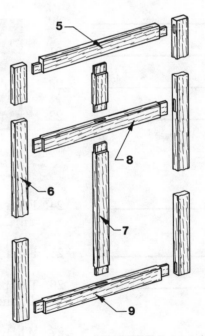

_____ 10. When panels are constructed of solid wood, the grooves in the stiles must be deeper than if the panels are of plywood or glued-up stock. (True or False)

_____ 11. The term used to describe the shape of the inside edge of the frame is ___ .

(Continued on next page)

99

Identify these types of inside edge.

_____ 12.

_____ 13.

_____ 14.

12

13

14

_____ 15. The frame parts are always joined by a mortise-and-tenon joint. (True or False)

_____ 16. Which type of panel is used most commonly on furniture doors?

Identify the kinds of panels in the illustrations.

_____ 17.

_____ 18.

_____ 19.

_____ 20.

_____ 21.

_____ 22.

_____ 23.

17

18

19

20

21

22

23

_____ 24. For a door that will have a glass panel, the frame must be cut with a(n) _____ around the inside edge.

_____ 25. For a $\frac{1}{4}$″ groove, the edges of the panel should be _____ thick.

_____ 26. The panel should be slightly less in overall dimensions than the distances to the bottom of the frame grooves. (True or False)

_____ 27. When assembling a panel and frame, glue should never be applied to the groove or to the panel. (True or False)

_____ 28. To cut a raised panel on a radial-arm saw, use a(n) _____ diameter blade.

_____ 29. When cutting a raised panel on a radial-arm saw, cut the edge grain first, then the end grain. (True or False)

_____ 30. Raised panel cutters can be used only on shapers with a $\frac{3}{4}$″ spindle. (True or False)

Unit 45
FURNITURE DOORS

(Text pages 603-623)

Match the material for case door construction on the left with the appropriate description.

_____   1. solid, glued-up stock

_____   2. tongue-and-groove panel-
                ing

_____   3. veneer-core plywood

_____   4. lumber-core plywood

_____   5. particle board

_____   6. hardboard

_____   7. glass

_____   8. honeycomb

A. base for doors covered with plastic laminate
B. needs special metal or plastic track
C. very lightweight
D. likely to warp
E. needs crosspieces
F. most common for kitchen cabinets built on-the-job
G. allows doors to be edge banded with same wood as face veneer
H. often used for small sliding doors

_____   9. Hardware for hanging a veneer-core plywood door must be edge-mounted. (True or False)

_____   10. Fine furniture and cabinets usually have ____ doors.

_____   11. ____ doors are made to slide in a track around a corner.

_____   12. Flush and lipped doors are two kinds of ____ ____ doors.

_____   13. The ____ ____ door covers the edges of the case or carcass.

_____   14. The ____ ____ door is made so that the door covers only part of the face frame, but needs no rabbet cuts.

_____   15. What type door is the most time-consuming to install?

(Continued on next page)

Match the type of hinge with the appropriate description.

_____ 16. wrap-around
_____ 17. continuous butt
_____ 18. semi-concealed
_____ 19. pivot
_____ 20. butt
_____ 21. double-action
_____ 22. surface

A. made with either fixed or loose pins; leaves may be straight or swaged
B. used on long or heavy doors; comes in lengths up to 72″
C. used for all types of cabinet doors and built-ins; often made to be self-closing
D. may be flat or offset; are mounted on front of door and case
E. used mainly for flush overlay doors; may be installed on vertical or horizontal surface
F. mainly for doors of plywood or particle board
G. ideal for shutters and folding doors

Identify the types of hinges illustrated.

_____ 23.
_____ 24.
_____ 25.
_____ 26.
_____ 27.

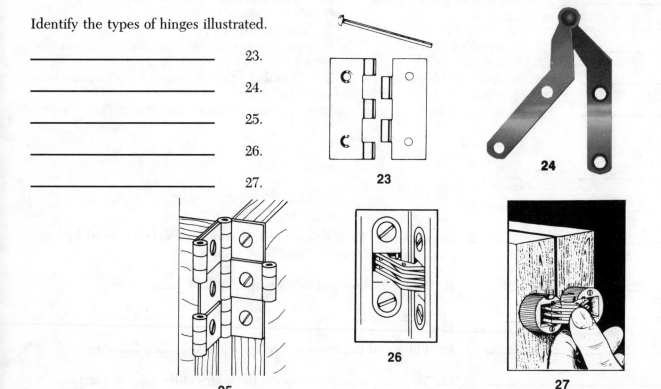

23

24

25

26

27

_____ 28. A flush door is always made ____ inch thinner than the frame.

_____ 29. One way to hang a pair of flush doors so that the crack between doesn't show is to cut a ____ on the front of the left door and on the back of the right door.

_____ 30. On a lip door, the lip overlaps the frame by ____ on all sides.

_____ 31. Reveal overlay doors overlap the opening by ____ on all sides.

_____ 32. For sliding doors, the top and bottom tracks must be the same depth. (True or False)

Date _____ Name _____

Score: (33 possible) _____

Unit 46
DRAWERS AND DRAWER GUIDES

(Text pages 624-648)

_____ 1. Drawer construction is an indicator of the quality of a furniture piece. (True or False)

_____ 2. The front of a _____ drawer is even with the frame.

_____ 3. The front of a _____ drawer covers part of the face plate, and a rabbet is cut on three or four sides of the drawer.

_____ 4. The front of the _____ _____ drawer covers the sides of the cabinet.

_____ 5. The front of the _____ _____ drawer covers part of the face frame.

_____ 6. The ends of the drawer front of flush drawers should be cut back _____ .

_____ 7. The front of a drawer must be made of solid wood. (True or False)

_____ 8. The material for the sides of drawers is usually _____ thick.

_____ 9. When a drawer is to have a side guide, the sides should be _____ thick.

_____ 10. Drawer sides are sometimes made much longer than the interior dimensions of the drawer itself. (True or False)

_____ 11. Material for drawer bottoms should be _____ thick.

_____ 12. In high-quality construction, the drawer bottom fits into a groove on all four surrounding members. (True or False)

Identify the joints for fastening drawer backs to sides.

_____ 13.

_____ 14.

_____ 15.

_____ 16.

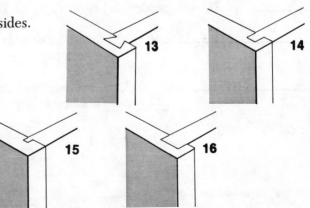

(Continued on next page)

Identify the joints for joining drawer fronts to sides.

_____ 17.

_____ 18.

_____ 19.

_____ 20.

_____ 21.

_____ 22.

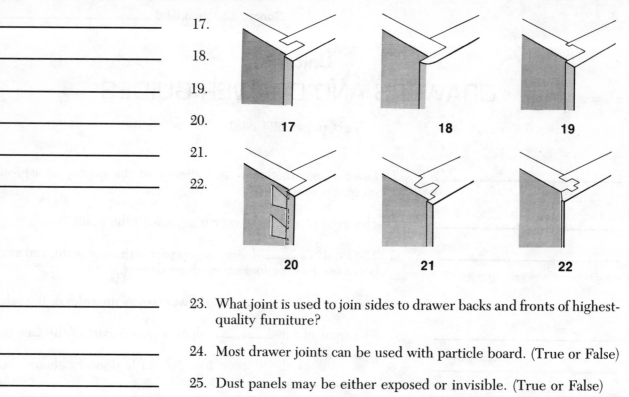

17   **18**   **19**

20   **21**   **22**

_____ 23. What joint is used to join sides to drawer backs and fronts of highest-quality furniture?

_____ 24. Most drawer joints can be used with particle board. (True or False)

_____ 25. Dust panels may be either exposed or invisible. (True or False)

_____ 26. A(n) _____ is a piece mounted above the sides of the drawer to keep it from tipping when it is pulled forward.

_____ 27. The groove for installing the drawer bottom should be at least _____ deep.

Match the drawer guides on the left with the descriptions on the right.

_____ 28. center guide and runners

_____ 29. runner for drawer sides

_____ 30. commercial drawer slides

_____ 31. side guides and runners

A. drawer sides fit into corner made by frame and sides

B. wood runner fastened to drawer bottom and guide fastened between front and back of frame

C. runner fastened to drawer sides; it slides in groove cut in sides of case

D. can be either side or bottom guides

_____ 32. Cut the sides about _____ narrower than the height of the drawer opening.

_____ 33. The completed drawer is slightly narrower in back than in the front. (True or False)

Unit 47
SHELVES AND CABINET INTERIORS

(Text pages 648-655)

_____   1. In built-ins of better quality, shelves are made of particle board or plywood. (True or False)

_____   2. Shelving that is unsupported for more than 42″ must be at least ____ thick.

Match the types of shelving with the appropriate description.

_____   3. standard book shelves

_____   4. upper kitchen cabinets

_____   5. lower kitchen cabinets

_____   6. upper bookcase shelves

_____   7. lower bookcase shelves

A. no less than 9½″ apart
B. no less than 12½″ apart
C. 8″ deep
D. 12″-14″ deep
E. 24″ deep
F. no less than 10″ deep

Identify the methods of installing stationary shelving shown in these illustrations.

_____   8.

_____   9.

_____   10.

_____   11.

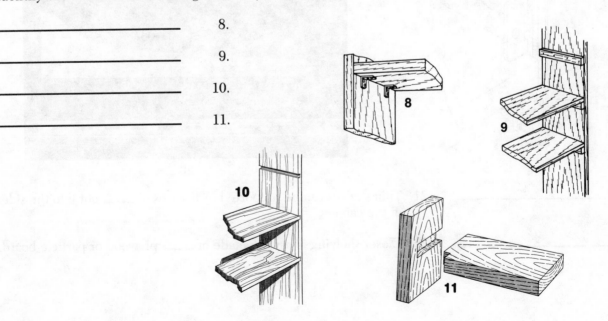

(Continued on next page)

_____ 12. One method of making adjustable shelving is to cut a series of oversized dadoes, equally spaced apart. (True or False)

_____ 13. Plastic and metal shelf pins require a drilled hole _____ in diameter.

_____ 14. The holes for shelf pins should be
   A. ½″ from the front and back edge.
   B. flush with the front and back edge.
   C. close to the center of the shelf.
   D. 1″ to 2″ from the front and back edges.
   E. any of the above, depending on what type of storage unit they will be used in.

_____ 15. Commercial shelf holders, such as plastic or metal shelf pins, are found on much high-quality furniture and cabinets. (True or False)

_____ 16. When using shelf standards, flush mounting provides a neater appearance. (True or False)

Identify the types of shelf hardware in the illustrations.

_____ 17.

_____ 18.

_____ 19.

_____ 20.

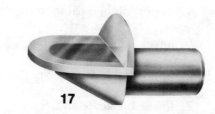

17

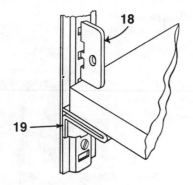

18

19

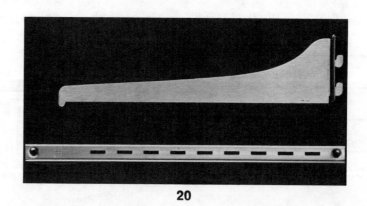

20

_____ 21. Thin shelves can be supported by a series of _____ cut into the sides of the cabinet.

_____ 22. Closet shelving is usually made of _____ plywood or particle board.

Unit 48
LEGS, POSTS, AND FEET

(Text pages 656-674)

_____ 1. Legs, posts, and feet should be made of solid lumber. (True or False)

_____ 2. The square, straight leg is commonly found on what style furniture?

_____ 3. When a taper is to be cut on two adjoining surfaces, one side should be laid out and cut before the second layout is made. (True or False)

_____ 4. Turned legs and posts are commonly found on Early American and Traditional furniture. (True or False)

_____ 5. On turned legs, the concave curve is called a(n) _____ .

_____ 6. On turned legs, the convex curve is called a(n) _____ .

_____ 7. Short, straight lines that separate different parts of a turned leg are called _____ .

_____ 8. A _____ joint is made by turning a spindle leg or rung slightly larger than the hole into which it is to fit and then running it through rollers to reduce its diameter.

_____ 9. The cabriole leg is characteristic of what period of furniture?

_____ 10. English designs emphasize what part of the cabriole leg?

_____ 11. What part of the cabriole leg do French designs emphasize?

_____ 12. What type top is used on a cabriole leg if it is to be attached to a rectangular or square table or chair?

_____ 13. What type top is used on a cabriole leg if it is to be used on a circular or oval chair?

_____ 14. A large rabbet cut out of the top of a cabriole leg is called a(n) ____ ____ .

_____ 15. You should glue up three pieces of stock to produce the rough material for each Queen Anne cabriole leg. (True or False)

_____ 16. Extra pieces of wood attached to the upper part of a cabriole leg are called wings or _____ .

(Continued on next page)

17. How are these wings attached to the leg?

18. The carved animal feet on some cabriole legs are best cut
    A. by hand with wood carving tools.
    B. with a model-maker's plane.
    C. with a carving attachment on a router.
    D. with special attachments on a shaper.

19. What type of foot is shown in this illustration?

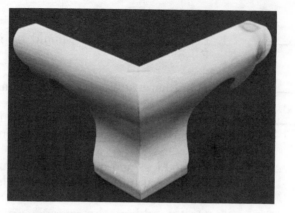

20. Stock used to make the type of foot in question 19 must be at least
    ____ inch(es) thick.

21. When making this type of foot, a ____ must be cut on the side
    opposite the curve on each of the pieces for the front feet.

22. These pieces for the front feet are then joined using a(n) ____ and
    glue.

23. A ____ ____ is attached to the side piece of each back foot of this
    type of leg.

24. ____ is a series of equally spaced convex divisions on a leg or post.

25. ____ is a series of equally spaced concave divisions on a leg or post.

26. To cut parallel V-shaped flutes on a flat surface, use a(n) ____
    ____ on a radial-arm saw.

27. Which of the following is *not* a common method for joining legs to
    a pedestal?
    A. dowel joint
    B. lock joint
    C. blind mortise-and-tenon joint
    D. dovetail dado joint

Unit 49
LEG-AND-RAIL CONSTRUCTION

(Text pages 675-684)

_____ 1. Leg-and-rail construction is also called _____ construction.

_____ 2. In table construction, another name for rail is _____ .

_____ 3. Lower rails on tables are called _____ .

_____ 4. When mortises are cut on two adjoining surfaces, such as on a table leg, the tenons must be mitered on the end. (True or False)

_____ 5. What joint is the traditional method of joining a leg to a rail?

_____ 6. What joint is a good choice for legs of furniture that is to be shipped unassembled?

_____ 7. What joint do makers of fine furniture today choose when they want strong, fast, and inexpensive leg-and-rail construction?

Identify these joints used in leg-and-rail construction.

_____ 8.
_____ 9.
_____ 10.
_____ 11.

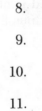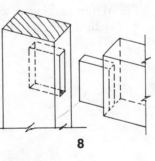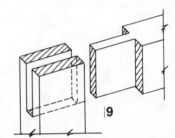

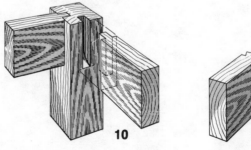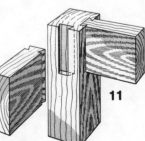

(Continued on next page)

_____

_____

_____

_____

_____

_____

_____

_____

_____

_____

12. For more strength, ____ ____ are used on the butt joint reinforced with dowels.

13. Butt joints cannot be used in leg-and-rail construction when the leg and rail are not at right angles to each other. (True or False)

14. In doweled leg-and-rail construction, the hole is bored exactly at right angles to the edge of the leg. (True or False)

15. When a drawer is installed right under the top of a table, an interior ____ ____ is usually installed for attaching drawer guides and for support.

16. One way to install a lower shelf on a table is to simply install a dowel at each corner. (True or False)

17. One way to install a lower shelf on a table is to cut a ____ ____ on the legs and then cut the shelf to fit.

18. What type of furniture is considered the most difficult to construct?

19. Chairs are usually designed with the front wider than the back. (True or False)

20. When making a mortise-and-tenon joint for the side rails of a chair,
    A. the tenon must be mitered at the end.
    B. the tenon must be reduced in width to fit the mortise.
    C. the tenon must be cut at the proper angle.
    D. the mortise should be cut deeper at the bottom than at the top.
    E. none of the above

21. When making a sculptured joint, extra material should be left on both the leg and the base, then final shaping is done after assembly. (True or False)

Unit 50
TABLETOPS

(Text pages 684-698)

_____   1. Tabletops should always be fastened permanently in place. (True or False)

_____   2. Plywood for tabletops is usually ____ thick.

_____   3. What is the major problem when using plywood for tabletops?

_____   4. Hardwood plywood tabletops can be either veneer-core or lumber-core. (True or False)

Match the kind of tabletop on the left with the appropriate description.

_____   5. plywood center with a band or frame

_____   6. softwood or hardwood plywood

_____   7. solid, glued-up stock

_____   8. core stock covered with plastic laminate

A. very subject to expansion and contraction
B. popular for tops of built-ins and tables; easy to keep clean
C. simplest way to build a top
D. will not warp; expands and contracts very little

_____   9. When a top has a plywood center with a band or frame, the band must match the plywood exactly. (True or False)

_____   10. Which of the following is *not* used to join the band to a plywood top?
    A. dowels
    B. spline
    C. tongue-and-groove joint
    D. butt edge

_____   11. How wide should the pieces be when gluing up solid wood for a large surface?

_____   12. When gluing up solid wood strips for a large surface, you should alternate the pieces so that the heart side is up on every other board. (True or False)

(Continued on next page)

111

_____   13. Use a router to cut grooves across the grain on the underside of a top made of solid, glued-up stock. (True or False)

_____   14. With a(n) ____ hinge, the leaves of a drop-leaf table drop down but extend beyond the top.

_____   15. With a(n) ____ hinge, the leaves drop below and in line with the edge of the tabletop.

_____   16. A(n) ____ joint on a drop leaf has a cove molding on the leaf that slides over the thumbnail molding on the top.

_____   17. Hinges for the joint in question 16 must have one long and one short leaf. (True or False)

_____   18. In a butterfly drop leaf, a(n) ____ ____ swings out to support the leaves.

_____   19. On a(n) ____ table, each leaf is supported by a swinging leg.

_____   20. In the table in question 19, the swinging leg is attached to a movable rail called a(n) ____ ____ .

_____   21. In a slide support, a(n) ____ is cut on both edges of the center board so it can slide on two fixed boards called bearers.

_____   22. What is the simplest and easiest method of supporting a drop leaf?

Identify these types of support for drop leaves.

_____   23.

_____   24.

_____   25.

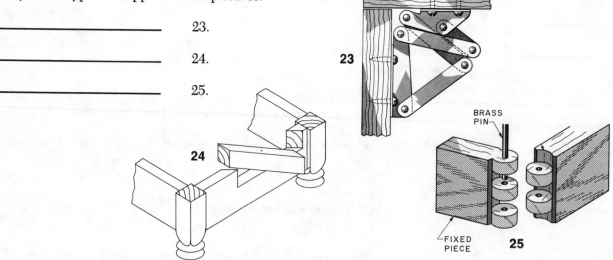

BRASS PIN

23

24

FIXED PIECE

25

_____   26. If a tabletop is made of solid wood, it must be fastened to the base very solidly and securely to keep it from warping. (True or False)

_____   27. One method of fastening solid wood tops to furniture is to use ____ blocks.

_____   28. What is the best method of fastening solid wood tabletops to furniture?

112

Unit 51
CASEWORK

(Text pages 699-721)

_____ 1. The undersides of wall cases that are four feet from the floor are considered exposed parts. (True or False)

_____ 2. Drawer sides and bottoms, the interior faces of doors, and shelves are all considered concealed parts in casework. (True or False)

_____ 3. The plywood chosen for most casework has a ____ core.

_____ 4. For solid lumber, the average movement due to humidity changes is plus or minus ____ per 12 inches of width.

_____ 5. If casework is made from solid, glued-up lumber, the web frame must be slightly narrower than the sides of the case. (True or False)

_____ 6. In premium grade construction, ____ ____ joints are always used for exposed shelf edges.

_____ 7. The recessed area below the bottom of the front of many kitchen cabinets is covered by a(n) ____ ____ , which is rabbeted on both ends to fasten over the cabinet sides.

_____ 8. Heavy wood pieces called ____ are placed on edge from front to back under the case to give extra support.

_____ 9. A(n) ____ is the lowest square or rectangular shape of a cabinet or furniture piece.

_____ 10. Which of the following is *not* among the best corner joints for casework?
A. spline miter
B. miter with a rabbet
C. rabbet
D. lock miter

_____ 11. If a case is to have a back, a(n) ____ should be cut around the inside of its back edges.

_____ 12. If the case is to fit against the wall, the cut around the inside back edges should be deeper than the thickness of the back. (True or False)

_____ 13. Plastic laminate tops for custom grade casework must be press glued. (True or False)

(Continued on next page)

14. In elementary drawer construction, the drawers can have extended bottoms which slide on _____ cut in the case sides.

15. Finest casework has a(n) _____ _____ to support the drawer.

16. Casework with drawers usually includes dust panels. (True or False)

17. The front of best-quality casework has a(n) _____ .

18. Which of the following is *not* a good joint for the corner of a faceplate or frame?
    A. stub mortise-and-tenon
    B. dowel
    C. haunched mortise-and-tenon
    D. miter with a rabbet

19. Staples have better holding power than nails. (True or False)

20. The cabinet top is usually not installed until the base cabinet is assembled, in place, and fastened to the wall. (True or False)

21. The most common grade of exterior finish for economy grade casework is _____ .

22. The illustrations below show a type of construction called _____ .

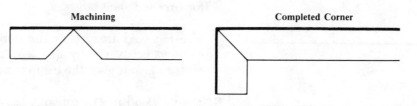

23. Rigid laminates such as wood veneers or plastic laminate cannot be used in the procedure in question 22. (True or False)

24. With _____ a stereo cabinet can be made from a single flat sheet of board.

25. No face frame is used on any cabinet constructed by the European system. (True or False)

26. In the European system, holes for dowels and fittings must be drilled in a precise _____ pattern.

27. What kind of joints are used in the European system?

28. The European system is efficient and cost-effective, but cabinets are not quite as strong as those made by traditional methods. (True or False)

29. _____ is the science used to design tools, machines, and equipment to fit the human body.

Unit 52
FINE FURNITURE CABINETWORK

(Text pages 722-737)

_____   1. In flush top construction, all the top, end, and base panels are the same thickness. (True or False)

Match the type of joint on the right to the parts each is used to join in flush top construction.

_____ 2. lock-miter

_____ 3. dado

_____ 4. rabbet

_____ 5. notched edge cross lap

A. base panel to end panel
B. vertical and horizontal parting rails
C. top to sides
D. dust frame to end panel

_____   6. The back horizontal rail is braced to the end panel with a(n) _____ ____ .

_____   7. In furniture cabinetwork, greater use is made of solid wood for legs, posts, and rails than in casework. (True or False)

_____   8. Sides, fronts, doors, and drawers for furniture cabinetwork commonly use _____ construction.

_____   9. Quality furniture has mortised joints on both the fronts and backs of drawers. (True or False)

_____   10. What type of joint is used on mirrors and door frames to add strength and minimize warpage?

_____   11. Since much of the construction is the same, tables, chairs, and beds are considered cabinetwork. (True or False)

_____   12. A lock-miter joint can be cut on a shaper with either a $\frac{1}{2}''$ or $\frac{3}{4}''$ spindle. (True or False)

_____   13. When cutting the first part of the lock-miter joint on the top of the cabinet, hold the work _____ .

_____   14. When cutting the second part of the lock-miter joint on the sides of the cabinet, hold the work _____ .

(Continued on next page)

15. A _____ joint is usually used to join the sides to the bottom of a cabinet or chest.

16. The typical chest of drawers consists of a case which is divided and held together by ___ ___ ___ .

17. Which of the following would *not* be a part of the base unit of cabinetwork?
    A. legs
    B. leg-and-rail construction
    C. plinth
    D. pediment

18. What type of corner joint is usually used in constructing a plinth?

19. The plinth is usually attached to the lower casework or cabinet with _____ on all four interior surfaces.

20. How high should a plinth be?

21. The _____ is a decorative terminal piece installed vertically to accent a point or the ending of a structure.

22. A(n) _____ is a projecting molding used to give an architectural finish to the top edge of a large cabinet, such as a china cabinet.

23. _____ are a series of small rectangular blocks projecting under a cornice.

Unit 53
KITCHEN CABINETS

(Text pages 738-761)

_____   1. The best-quality kitchen cabinets are produced to the same standards as fine furniture. (True or False)

_____   2. Of all kitchen cabinets, probably the base unit requires the greatest sturdiness. (True or False)

_____   3. The best height for the base unit is ____ from the floor.

_____   4. In planning the layout for a remodeled kitchen, measurements must be accurate to ____ inch.

_____   5. Which type of kitchen arrangement makes the best allowance for having a dining area within the kitchen?

Match the items on the left with the dimensions on the right.

_____   6. depth of wall cabinets   A. 18″ to 36″
                                              B. 16″

_____   7. clearance between center of front burner and wall or high equipment unit   C. 12″ to 24″
       D. 12″ to 14″
       E. 24″ to 36″

_____   8. counter space to left of sink

_____   9. counter space to right of sink

_____   10. width of base unit on either side of surface cooking area

_____   11. If there is a dishwasher, allow ____ for it when planning the kitchen arrangement.

_____   12. The standard clearance between the countertop and the bottom of a wall cabinet is ____ inches.

_____   13. Always install ____ cabinets first.

(Continued on next page)

_____   14. If the floor slopes away from the wall, you can make base cabinets level by trimming off the base at an angle to fit the floor. (True or False)

_____   15. Base cabinets are fastened to the walls with ____ ____ .

_____   16. Cabinets that are installed side by side should be bolted together. (True or False)

_____   17. When installing a wall cabinet, use ____ ____ if the wall is uneven and out of plumb.

_____   18. Cabinets built piece by piece on-the-job need no backs. (True or False)

_____   19. Non-frame cabinet construction uses no solid wood. (True or False)

_____   20. Non-frame cabinets with overlap drawers and doors do not need a face frame. (True or False)

_____   21. Base and sink units for a bathroom are about ____ tall.

_____   22. How deep are base and sink units for a bathroom?
    A. 24 inches
    B. 30 inches
    C. 16 to 21 inches
    D. 22 to 26 inches
    E. 28 inches

Unit 54
PANELING

(Text pages 761-769)

_____ 1. Molding used as trim between two different types of wall finish is called ____ .

_____ 2. Solid wood paneling has ____ joints for assembling the boards.

_____ 3. Solid wood paneling comes in widths from 4" to ____ .

_____ 4. Furring strips should be spaced at least ____ apart.

_____ 5. More, but narrower, furring strips are needed for nailing ¼" plywood than for nailing solid wood paneling. (True or False)

_____ 6. Furring strips are not used when paneling is to be applied to a wood frame. (True or False)

_____ 7. When applying furring strips to a plastered wall, use ____ ____ .

_____ 8. Furring strips must be straight and true. (True or False)

_____ 9. When nailing solid wood paneling to furring strips, use ____ nails.

_____ 10. When paneling is not to extend the full height of the wall, it can be installed without using any nails. (True or False)

_____ 11. It is a good idea to use both horizontal and vertical furring strips when installing plywood panels. (True or False)

_____ 12. If there are several windows and doors, start paneling at one corner and work your way around the room. (True or False)

_____ 13. What type of joint is preferred for joining plywood paneling?

_____ 14. One good method of fastening plywood paneling to a wall is a combination of small brads and spot gluing. (True or False)

_____ 15. When nailing plywood paneling, be sure to first put a nail in each top corner to hold the board in place. (True or False)

_____ 16. In inside corners, panels are usually joined with a(n) ____ ____ .

_____ 17. What kind of molding is used on an inside corner?

_____ 18. Fill all nail holes before applying any sealer. (True or False)

Unit 55
BUILT-INS, INCLUDING ROOM DIVIDERS

(Text pages 770-781)

_____ 1. With mill- or shop-built cabinets, the work is checked with a ____ .

_____ 2. With built-ins, much of the work must be checked with a ____ .

_____ 3. Which of the following is *not* true of built-ins?
A. They simplify housecleaning.
B. They often must be made to fit irregular surfaces.
C. They offer a customer-built appearance.
D. They are built according to an architect's plans.

_____ 4. Nearly all bedroom furnishings can be built-in. (True or False)

_____ 5. Humidity problems limit the use of built-ins in bathrooms. (True or False)

_____ 6. Before constructing a built-in, check the ____ for levelness.

_____ 7. Also check the ____ to see if it is perpendicular.

_____ 8. Check the ____ to see whether they are out-of-square.

_____ 9. Check the wall studs and ____ ____ to know where the built-in will be fastened in place.

_____ 10. Join horizontal frames, such as for drawers, with ____ ____ .

Arrange these steps for constructing a built-in in the proper order.

_____ 11. First step
_____ 12. Second step
_____ 13. Third step
_____ 14. Fourth step
_____ 15. Fifth step
_____ 16. Sixth step
_____ 17. Final step

A. Adjust the main horizontal pieces to the distance from side to side.
B. Build the doors and drawers and fit them in place.
C. Install the intermediate pieces.
D. Make out a complete materials list.
E. Shim the horizontal and vertical pieces to make sure they are plumb and level.
F. Adjust the main vertical pieces to the overall ceiling height.
G. Build the interior, including shelves, dividers, and other parts.

Unit 56
PREPARATION FOR FINISHING

(Text pages 786-792)

_____ 1. Which of the following is *not* always done in preparation for finishing?
  A. removing any surface glue
  B. repairing dents and scratches
  C. final sanding
  D. bleaching

_____ 2. Any imperfection or scratch left after final sanding will be greatly intensified when the final finish is applied. (True or False)

_____ 3. Glue around joints can be removed with a(n) ____ ____ .

_____ 4. Any glue that has spilled and dried on the surface can be removed by sanding. (True or False)

_____ 5. A shallow dent can be raised with a wet cloth and a(n) ____ ____ .

_____ 6. A good way to fill small cracks is to use heated ____ ____ .

_____ 7. The repair method in question 6 is called the ____ method.

_____ 8. When applying wood putty or plastic wood to fill a crack or hole, make sure the filler is level with the surface, then allow it to dry. (True or False)

_____ 9. A good way to cover screw holes is with ____ ____ .

_____ 10. A mild bleach solution is made by mixing ____ ____ in hot water.

_____ 11. The strongest bleach is made by mixing equal parts of caustic soda and concentrated ____ ____ .

_____ 12. What solution is used to wash off the residue the bleach leaves on the wood surface?

_____ 13. When washing off the bleached surface, it is a good idea to apply plain water to the opposite face. (True or False)

(Continued on next page)

_____ 14. Wood bleaches are inflammable and must be used away from any open flame or spark, as well as in a well-ventilated area. (True or False)

_____ 15. No eye protection is necessary when bleaching. (True or False)

_____ 16. Which of the following types of containers should *not* be used when mixing bleach?
A. stainless steel
B. glass
C. aluminum
D. ceramic

_____ 17. Apply the bleach solution with a cellulose sponge or a(n) ____ ____ .

_____ 18. Allow the bleach solution to remain on the surface about ____ ____ .

_____ 19. Allow the bleached surface to dry at least ____ ____ after rinsing before proceeding with any further finishing steps.

_____ 20. If a transparent finish is to be applied to casework or a built-in, final sanding should be done with ____ ____ paper.

_____ 21. Just before final sanding, a(n) ____ ____ can be applied to the wood to make the surface fibers more firm.

_____ 22. This mixture consists of one gallon warm water to one-fourth pound of ____ ____ ____ .

_____ 23. Generally speaking, the surface of a piece of furniture should be sanded with what grade and mineral of abrasive paper?

_____ 24. After final sanding, wipe the surface clean with a(n) ____ ____ .

Unit 57
FINISHING EQUIPMENT AND SUPPLIES

(Text pages 793-804)

_____ 1. The ____ ____ takes the air at atmospheric pressure and delivers it to the spray gun at a higher pressure.

_____ 2. The ____ ____ removes oil, dirt, and moisture from the air going to the gun.

_____ 3. The ____ -fed gun is best when an extra-fine finish is desired.

_____ 4. A container is directly mounted on the ____ -fed gun.

Identify the numbered parts of this suction-fed spray gun.

_____ 5.

_____ 6.

_____ 7.

_____ 8.

_____ 9.

_____ 10.

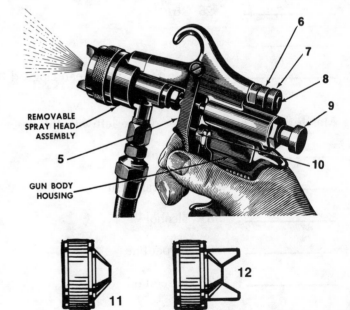

Identify the two types of spray nozzles.

_____ 11.

_____ 12.

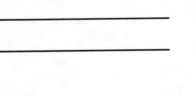

_____ 13. For spraying lacquer use the ____ -mix gun.

_____ 14. The ____ -type gun has a valve which shuts off the air when the trigger is released.

_____ 15. To apply lacquer with a portable spray gun, use the lacquer full-strength. (True or False)

(Continued on next page)

_____   16. The spray pattern is controlled by the ___ ___ ___.

_____   17. If the spray is too fine, increase the pressure. (True or False)

_____   18. How far should the gun be held from the surface being sprayed?

_____   19. Control the spray stroke with wrist movement. (True or False)

_____   20. The gun should be kept at a ___ angle to the surface at all points along the stroke.

_____   21. Strokes should be overlapped about ___ per cent.

Match the spray problems on the left with the descriptions on the right.

_____   22. mist or fog

_____   23. sandy finish

_____   24. starving

_____   25. runs

_____   26. streaks

_____   27. sags

      A. not enough air or fluid reaching gun
      B. caused by tipping gun up or down
      C. fluid too thin or air pressure too high
      D. too much fluid has been applied
      E. gun too far away
      F. spray material too thin

_____   28. Clean clogged holes with a sharp nail or wire. (True or False)

Match the finishing supplies on the left with the descriptions on the right.

_____   29. rottenstone

_____   30. mineral spirits

_____   31. alcohol

_____   32. turpentine

_____   33. linseed oil

_____   34. benzene

      A. will do everything turpentine will do
      B. ingredient in paints, fillers and stains
      C. used after pumice
      D. thinner and solvent for shellac
      E. solvent and cleaning fluid made from coal tar
      F. solvent for paint, enamel, and varnish

_____   35. ___ is a white-colored powder combined with water or oil to rub down the finish.

_____   36. When applying finish, dip the brush into the finishing material about ___ the bristle length.

124

Unit 58
FINISHING PROCEDURES

(Text pages 804-811)

_____ 1. A truly high-quality finish requires many steps. (True or False)

_____ 2. The natural color of many woods can be changed by ____ .

_____ 3. Color variations in wood can be evened out by ____ ____ .

_____ 4. Which of the following is *not* true of staining?
A. It changes the tone.
B. It emphasizes the grain.
C. It adds color.
D. It helps preserve the wood.

_____ 5. To keep the stain from bleeding into the finish, apply a ____ ____ .

_____ 6. The material needed for the step in question 5 can be made by mixing seven parts alcohol to ____ ____ ____ ____ ____ .

_____ 7. ____ add color and close the pores of the wood.

_____ 8. Closed-grain woods do not need to have the material in question 7 applied. (True or False)

_____ 9. A(n) ____ ____ is needed to close the pores in oak and walnut.

_____ 10. ____ is done to give a highlighted, shaded, or antique effect.

(Continued on next page)

Arrange these step for finishing open-grained wood in the proper sequence.

———————————— 11. First step

———————————— 12. Second step

———————————— 13. Third step

———————————— 14. Fourth step

———————————— 15. Fifth step

———————————— 16. Sixth step

———————————— 17. Seventh step

———————————— 18. Eighth step

———————————— 19. Last step

A. Apply colored filler; allow to dry.
B. Rub with paste wax.
C. Apply three coats of lacquer.
D. Apply a glue size; allow to dry; sand.
E. Rub with pumice and water.
F. Apply sealer coat of shellac or lacquer; allow to dry; sand.
G. Apply a wash coat of shellac or lacquer; allow to dry; sand.
H. Apply a glaze, if desired.
I. Apply water stain; allow to dry; sand.

Match the commercial synthetic finishes on the left with the descriptions on the right.

———————————— 20. Sealacell

———————————— 21. Varno wax

———————————— 22. Royal Finish

———————————— 23. Minwax

———————————— 24. Danish oil

———————————— 25. Deft

A. penetrating wood seal and wax; applied directly to raw wood
B. final coat; can have deep luster or soft egg-shell finish
C. blend of gums and waxes
D. applied directly to raw wood; can be mixed with stain or filler
E. semi-gloss, clear finish; seals, primes, and finishes wood
F. combines with wood chemically to seal, prime, finish, and preserve it; flat finish

———————————— 26. One disadvantage of Danish oil finishes is that they cannot be easily repaired. (True or False)

———————————— 27. Which of the following is *not* true of a shellac finish?
A. adds no tone at all
B. clear finish
C. good for close-grained woods
D. good if wood is to be exposed to moisture

———————————— 28. Which of the following is *not* true of a natural oil finish?
A. short drying time between coats
B. preserves the wood
C. grows darker with time
D. Additional coats can be applied as needed, even a year later.

———————————— 29. What style furniture is commonly given a natural oil finish?

Unit 59
STAINING

(Text pages 811-820)

_____ 1. Stains can be used to make a less expensive wood look like a costly one. (True or False)

_____ 2. When sapwood and heartwood differ greatly in color, the wood should be ____ ____ before it is stained.

_____ 3. ____ ____ are finely ground color particles that disperse, but do not dissolve, in the vehicle for the stain.

_____ 4. Wood treated with ____ stain shows greater contrast in figure than wood treated with other stains.

_____ 5. ____ stains raise the grain of the wood.

_____ 6. When exposed to sunlight, oil stains bleach more than water stains. (True or False)

_____ 7. Generally, the mixture of water stains is ____ ____ of powder to one gallon of water.

_____ 8. The color of water stains will appear darker on a small test piece than on a large surface. (True or False)

_____ 9. Always sponge ____ ____ with water just before applying water stain.

_____ 10. Water stains are commonly used in industrial finishing. (True or False)

_____ 11. Stains that consist of color mixed in boiled linseed oil and turpentine are called ____ stains.

_____ 12. Which of the following woods should *not* be given a pigment-oil stain?
A. maple
B. oak
C. birch
D. beech
E. gum

(Continued on next page)

_____ 13. When using oil stains, apply linseed oil to the ___ ___ before staining.

_____ 14. Penetrating-oil stains are commonly given a lacquer finish. (True or False)

_____ 15. Penetrating-oil stains do not bleed or fade. (True or False)

_____ 16. ___ stains are made by dissolving soluble dyes in alcohol.

_____ 17. Which of the following is *not* true of the stains in question 16?
A. fast-drying
B. penetrate deeply
C. tend to bleed
D. may need two coats for dark shades

_____ 18. Non-grain-raising stains do not fade or bleed. (True or False)

_____ 19. Non-grain-raising stains are applied by ___ .

_____ 20. Lacquer toners have very good staining properties. (True or False)

_____ 21. Which of the following is *not* a function of wash coating?
A. keep stain from bleeding
B. improve toughness of finish
C. keep stain from fading
D. provide hard surface for applying filler

_____ 22. A wash coat must be applied thickly. (True or False)

Unit 60
FILLING

(Text pages 816-820)

_____ 1. Use a light-colored filler with a very dark stain for a finish.

_____ 2. Which of the following would *not* require a paste filler?
　　　　　　　　　A. mahogany
　　　　　　　　　B. cherry
　　　　　　　　　C. hickory
　　　　　　　　　D. walnut

_____ 3. Paste filler must be applied both with and across the grain. (True or False)

_____ 4. Apply more filler to end grain. (True or False)

_____ 5. Paste filler should dry about ___ ___ before removing excess.

_____ 6. Do not pack filler tightly into pores. (True or False)

_____ 7. Apply liquid fillers the same way as paste fillers. (True or False)

_____ 8. Which of the following is *not* generally used with a liquid filler?
　　　　　　　　　A. birch
　　　　　　　　　B. redwood
　　　　　　　　　C. poplar
　　　　　　　　　D. beech

Match the defects on the left with the descriptions on the right.

_____ 9. pinholing
_____ 10. flow-out
_____ 11. bleeding
_____ 12. graying

　　　A. binder absorbed by wood or wrong filler used
　　　B. air bubbles show on surface
　　　C. filler squeezes out of pores as result of poor wash coat
　　　D. good sealer not applied over filler

_____ 13. A sealer should not be used unless the wood has first been filled. (True or False)

_____ 14. Which of the following is *not* a function of a sealer?
　　　　　　　　　A. form a barrier coat over the filler
　　　　　　　　　B. prevent wood from absorbing moisture
　　　　　　　　　C. provide foundation for the topcoats
　　　　　　　　　D. fill the pores

Unit 61

DISTRESSING, GLAZING, AND OTHER OVERTONE TREATMENTS

(Text pages 820-822)

_____   1. Most overtone treatments are applied after the filler and sealer have been applied. (True or False)

_____   2. Applying planned imperfections to a wood surface with chains, hammers, or coral rock is called ____ ____ .

_____   3. French and Italian Provincial furniture is often given a ____ finish to imitate the appearance of age and wear.

_____   4. ____ is done to give a furniture piece a highlighted, shaded, or antique appearance.

_____   5. Glaze for a painted or enameled surface is very thin and tends to run and drip. (True or False)

_____   6. Glaze should be applied to the entire surface, including dents and scratches. (True or False)

_____   7. It usually takes about ____ ____ for the glaze to set up.

_____   8. Rub the glaze off thoroughly and evenly. (True or False)

_____   9. It makes little difference what type or texture of material is used to do the wiping. (True or False)

_____   10. Allow ____ ____ for the glaze to dry completely.

_____   11. Further highlighting can be done with abrasive paper or ____ ____ .

_____   12. If a glaze has been applied, no topcoat is needed for a durable finish. (True or False)

_____   13. Adding darker glaze around edges or corners is called ____ .

_____   14. A speckled texture on the surface is achieved by a process called ____ .

_____   15. Imitation worm holes can be produced by ____ .

130

Unit 62
PROTECTIVE COATINGS

(Text pages 822-828)

_____   1. The most practical topcoat for the small cabinet shop is ____ ____ .

_____   2. Lacquers differ greatly from one manufacturer to another. (True or False)

_____   3. You must use the same brand of lacquer thinner as you do lacquer. (True or False)

_____   4. If lacquer contains too many solids and is sprayed cold, a(n) ____ ____ results.

_____   5. Which of the following is *not* true of lacquer finishes?
A. fast-drying
B. durable
C. may peel when exposed to excessive moisture
D. difficult to repair

_____   6. Lacquer for metal finishing is the same as that for wood finishing. (True or False)

_____   7. The final sheen of a lacquer coat can be changed greatly by the amount of rubbing and polishing done after application. (True or False)

_____   8. How far should the spray gun be held from the work when spraying lacquer?

_____   9. Use a(n) ____ stain when lacquer is to be brushed on.

_____   10. The best type of brush for applying lacquer is a(n) ____ brush.

_____   11. After dipping the brush in the lacquer, gently wipe it on the side of the container to remove excess. (True or False)

_____   12. Brush the lacquer in like paint. (True or False)

_____   13. Allow lacquer to dry ____ ____ before brushing on another coat.

_____   14. Varnish is commonly used in furniture production today. (True or False)

(Continued on next page)

_____ 15. _____ _____ varnish is quick-drying and water-resistant.

_____ 16. A good brush to use with varnish is a(n) _____ _____ , because it reduces the chance of bubbling.

_____ 17. Which of the following is *not* correct procedure when applying varnish?
A. Stir the varnish first.
B. Brush first across, then with the grain.
C. Apply sparingly.
D. Do a small area at a time.

_____ 18. Varnish should always be thinned before using. (True or False)

_____ 19. How long should varnish be allowed to dry between coats?

_____ 20. Polyurethane is the hardest and toughest finish available. (True or False)

_____ 21. A polyurethane finish is brittle and difficult to sand. (True or False)

_____ 22. Polyurethane is a good finish for furniture that will be exposed to frequent changes in humidity. (True or False)

_____ 23. If a surface has been varnished, allow it to dry for _____ _____ before final rubbing and polishing.

_____ 24. For best results, how long should a lacquer finish be allowed to dry before rubbing and polishing?

_____ 25. _____ is a burnishing action that removes or blends together fine scratch patterns.

_____ 26. Polishing is done with a _____ _____ attached to a wood block.

Match the finishes on the left with the techniques on the right.

_____ 27. high-sheen satin   A. rubbing; polishing with pumice and oil; cleaning; waxing

_____ 28. dull satin   B. rubbing; polishing with pumice and oil; polishing with rottenstone and oil

_____ 29. deep luster   C. rubbing; cleaning

_____ 30. period satin   D. rubbing; buffer polishing; cleaning; applying lemon-oil furniture polish

Unit 63
INTERIOR FINISHING

(Text pages 829-833)

_____ 1. Paneling is installed by either a rough or a finish carpenter. (True or False)

_____ 2. What should be used to fill nail holes, cracks, and gouges?

_____ 3. All paneling requires a filler. (True or False)

_____ 4. All paneling should be sealed. (True or False)

_____ 5. How many coats of topcoat should be applied?

_____ 6. After the last coat of finish, rub down with ___ ___ ___ .

_____ 7. Which of the following should *not* be done when producing a yellow color effect on rough-sawn paneling?
     A. Apply thick layer of yellow paint.
     B. Scrape off while finish is still wet.
     C. Allow knot-and-grain figuration to show through.
     D. Apply surface finish.
     E. All of the above steps should be followed.

_____ 8. Finish hardwood plywood interiors using the same procedures as you would for a piece of furniture. (True or False)

_____ 9. Which of the following would *not* be appropriate for a Traditional finish on mahogany paneling?
     A. Stain or leave natural.
     B. Apply filler.
     C. Apply lacquer.
     D. Apply high-gloss varnish.

_____ 10. For Contemporary interiors, especially with furniture that has a commercial oil finish, apply a(n) ___ finish.

_____ 11. For a natural finish on woods such as maple and birch, apply three coats of a synthetic ___ ___ .

_____ 12. How long should a penetrating finish be allowed to remain on the wood before wiping?

_____ 13. If penetration doesn't seem uniform, apply a second coat of penetrating finish before the first coat dries. (True or False)

(Continued on next page)

_____   14. Whatever finishing system is used for interiors of hardwood plywood, it should be pre-tested by *completely* finishing a small piece of that plywood. (True or False)

_____   15. When painting softwood plywood, any scratches or dents should be filled before undercoating. (True or False)

_____   16. For the undercoat, paint may be thinned to improve brushability. (True or False)

_____   17. Two undercoats are required for a painted finish on softwood plywood. (True or False)

_____   18. Undercoats should be tinted so they are about the same shade as the topcoat when painting softwood plywood. (True or False)

_____   19. In ____ ____ , stain and sealer are mixed together and applied in a single operation.

_____   20. Colored lacquer can be sprayed, brushed, or wiped on. (True or False)

_____   21. Rub a lacquer finish with ____ ____ between coats.

_____   22. A light ____ provides a natural finish which mellows a contrasting wood-grain pattern with warm colors.

_____   23. To provide a wearing surface on the finish in question 22, apply one coat of flat varnish or ____ ____ .

Unit 64
FURNITURE RESTORATION

(Text pages 833-852)

_____ 1. You may need to scrape a few small areas on the underside of a piece of old furniture to identify the type of wood. (True or False)

_____ 2. The term ____ means that a finish is cracked into large segments.

_____ 3. What products can be mixed to make a cleaner/conditioner?

_____ 4. What material is preferred for applying paste wax?

_____ 5. Use a(n) ____ to rub cleaner into carving and grooves.

_____ 6. After cleaning furniture that has dried out, apply a greaseless furniture cream containing ____ .

_____ 7. Over 90 per cent of the furniture that needs refinishing will have a shellac or lacquer finish. (True or False)

_____ 8. The finish is ____ if denatured alcohol will soften or remove it.

_____ 9. The finish is ____ if it is crystal hard and chips easily.

_____ 10. The finish is ____ if turpentine or mineral spirits will not soften it.

_____ 11. High-quality finish removers often contain the solvent ____ .

_____ 12. What is used to remove varnish?

_____ 13. Stroke finish remover on as you would paint. (True or False)

_____ 14. Lift off the sludge with a(n) ____ ____ .

_____ 15. If the remover is *not* water-soluble, the last residue can be removed by scrubbing the surface with steel wool dipped in ____ ____ .

_____ 16. To remove any remaining reddish stains from mahogany, apply full-strength ____ ____ .

_____ 17. Electric heat gun strippers are very good for removing old finish from fine furniture. (True or False)

_____ 18. The safest and best commercial method of stripping fine furniture is ____ ____ .

(Continued on next page)

135

_____

19. Use _____ _____ to soften old glue so that it can be removed.

_____

20. When regluing joints, it is not necessary to remove all the glue from the end grain. (True or False)

_____

21. If the crack in a split chair rung runs nearly the entire length, glue alone will not hold it together and additional support will be needed. (True or False)

_____

22. If a rung is only slightly loose in its socket, wrap _____ around the rung, then coat it with adhesive.

_____

23. You can place _____ _____ in the form of a cross over the end of a round or square joint to add thickness to the piece before gluing.

_____

24. Use a piece of _____ _____ to plug a hole that has become enlarged.

_____

25. Drilling a ⅛″ hole through the leg and the turned end of a rung, then inserting a glue-coated dowel is called _____ .

_____

26. To widen a round piece so it will fit snugly into a hole, cut a kerf into the end of the piece and insert a _____ _____ .

_____

27. To tighten a mortise-and-tenon joint, apply glue and insert a(n) _____ .

_____

28. The best method of repairing and strengthening loose joints in overstuffed furniture is with _____ _____ _____ .

_____

29. In the heat and water treatment for warped tops, you dampen the _____ side of the board and dry out the other side with heat.

_____

30. For some warped tops it may be necessary to cut a series of saw kerfs that run _____ the grain.

_____

31. How far apart should these kerfs be?

_____

32. What is inserted into these kerfs?

_____

33. To secure repaired tops to table frames, install _____ _____ at the joints between the top and frame, at each end, and along the sides.

_____

34. When reassembling a drawer, be sure to apply glue to the edge of the bottom. (True or False)

_____

35. A minor abrasion on a shellac surface can often be removed by brushing _____ on the damaged area.

_____

36. The lengthwise ends of a wood patch must be cut at a _____ _____ to the grain.

_____

37. When a shallow patch is glued in place, its upper surface should be slightly higher than the surrounding area. (True or False)

_____

38. What type of glue is used to reattach veneer?

Unit 65
WOODWORKING MANUFACTURING

(Text pages 855-894)

_____ 1. When lumber arrives at a furniture manufacturer, it must be air-dried for several months and then kiln-dried. (True or False)

_____ 2. The furniture designer makes the furniture models. (True or False)

_____ 3. Engineering working drawings are drawn to scale. (True or False)

_____ 4. During production, each part of a furniture piece is accompanied by a detail drawing and a ____ ____ .

_____ 5. If furniture manufacturers decide not to build all the parts themselves, they purchase them from a ____ manufacturer.

_____ 6. In the cutting room, or ____ ____ , pieces are cut to specific thickness, length, and width and natural defects caused by nature or drying are removed.

_____ 7. In furniture manufacture, the ____ is used to produce one surface that is flat and true.

_____ 8. The ____ ____ is used to cut thick stock to thinner pieces.

_____ 9. The ____ ____ is used to surface both sides of a board at the same time.

_____ 10. The ____ ____ trues up the edge of stock to make it ready for gluing.

_____ 11. ____ ____ ____ are high-production machines that apply glue, clamp stock together as it moves along, and dry the glue.

_____ 12. Lumber-core plywood for furniture usually has ____ plies.

_____ 13. Veneer ____ ____ ____ are used to cut veneer to size.

_____ 14. Glued edges of veneer are joined electrically with a ____ ____ ____ .

_____ 15. If solid wood must be bent, it must first be softened in a ____ ____ .

(Continued on next page)

137

_____ 16. On the automatic shaping lathe, the cutterhead rotates at a high speed and the stock rotates at a low speed. (True or False)

_____ 17. A pattern must be made on the hand lathe for use on the automatic shaping lathe. (True or False)

Match the machines in the left column with the proper description.

_____ 18. molder

_____ 19. double-end tenoner

_____ 20. double-spindle shaper

_____ 21. automatic profile shaper

_____ 22. contour profiler

_____ 23. automatic shaping lathe

_____ 24. single-spindle carver

A. can produce every kind of irregularly-shaped part

B. operator holds workpiece against the cutter freehand

C. has four cutterheads that rotate to make all kinds of cuts on straight stock

D. cuts lock joints and four-corner notches

E. makes it possible to cut with the grain at all times when cutting curves

F. floating cutterhead follows pattern to cut straight-line or curved pieces

G. cutterhead extends full length of stock and has a variety of knives

_____ 25. _____ sanders do the initial white-wood sanding as soon as the stock comes from the planer.

_____ 26. _____ sanders perform a wide range of operations, from simple curvatures to intricately shaped edges.

_____ 27. _____ sanders do inside sanding such as grille work.

_____ 28. The _____ sander is used on concave surfaces of irregularly-shaped moldings.

_____ 29. Most upholstery processes are still done by hand. (True or False)

_____ 30. The _____ _____ is where hand decorating is done and where hardware that has been removed for finishing is replaced.

_____ 31. Design changes on fronts of kitchen cabinets are often made by _____ _____ .

_____ 32. In the future more and more furniture products will be manufactured knocked down. (True or False)

_____ 33. _____ _____ _____ is a means of directing all functions of a machine automatically by predetermined instructions stored in a computer.

_____ 34. Robots can apply a uniform finish to furniture and cabinets. (True or False)

_____ 35. _____ are high-tech tools that can be used in woodworking for cutting, drilling, and engraving.

Unit 66

STORE, OFFICE, AND INSTITUTIONAL FIXTURES

(Text pages 895-912)

_____ 1. Which of the following is *not* true of the way fixture manufacture differs from furniture manufacture?
A. There is greater variation in size and shape with fixtures.
B. Fixtures are made of many things besides wood.
C. The size and shape of fixtures are not specified by customer demand.
D. Fixtures are often built around electrical and plumbing needs.

_____ 2. Cabinetmakers are not employed by fixture manufacturers. (True or False)

_____ 3. Which of the following is *not* a characteristic of fixtures?
A. built for rugged use
B. low in maintenance and upkeep
C. low cost
D. hardware usually metal
E. All of the above are characteristics of fixtures.

_____ 4. Wood wall cases have the same basic parts as a large china cabinet might have. (True or False)

_____ 5. Doors on wood wall cases usually have ____ construction or flush construction.

_____ 6. Drawers for wall cases have ____ construction between the front and sides.

_____ 7. The long central shelving units in supermarkets are called ____ .

_____ 8. What type of paneling is best suited to public places?

_____ 9. When joining panels with the ____ system, a groove and rabbet are cut in both edges.

_____ 10. Before installing paneling, install ____ ____ horizontally to the walls.

_____ 11. Where is the first panel installed?

_____ 12. Use ____ ____ nails to install this paneling.

_____ 13. Usually the wall cabinets and cases are installed before paneling. (True or False)

Unit 67
METRIC MEASUREMENT IN CABINETMAKING

(Text pages 913-926)

_____ 1. About 90 per cent of the world's people use the ____ system of measurement.

_____ 2. The term *kilo* means ____ ____ .

_____ 3. What is the customary equivalent of one metre in inches?

_____ 4. A metre rule is divided into 100 equal parts called ____ .

_____ 5. What is the customary fractional equivalent of one millimetre?

_____ 6. A kilogram equals approximately ____ pound(s).

_____ 7. One ounce equals approximately ____ grams.

_____ 8. A litre is slightly larger than a ____ .

_____ 9. A litre of water weighs ____ kilogram(s).

_____ 10. On the Celsius scale, water freezes at ____ degrees.

_____ 11. ____ ____ means converting existing dimensions to their metric equivalents.

_____ 12. ____ ____ means changing the dimensions to conform to metric standards.

_____ 13. A 2″ x 4″ would have a nominal metric dimension of ____ .

_____ 14. One inch equals approximately ____ millimetre(s).

_____ 15. Approximately how many centimeters are there in one foot?

_____ 16. What is the customary equivalent of 10mm?

_____ 17. What is the customary equivalent of one kilometre?

Unit 68
KINDS AND USES OF PLASTICS

(Text pages 930-940)

_____   1. The word ____ is commonly used to mean the same thing as plastics.

_____   2. What type of plastics become soft when heated and hard when cooled, regardless of how often the heating-cooling process is repeated?

_____   3. Thermosetting plastics are less resistant to damage caused by high temperatures than thermoplastics. (True or False)

_____   4. Thermoplastics are an excellent recycling material, while thermosetting plastics cannot be recycled. (True or False)

_____   5. Almost all finishing materials, including paints and stains, are made from plastics. (True or False)

Match the kind of plastic on the left with the description on the right.

_____   6. ABS plastic

_____   7. acrylic

_____   8. polyester resin

_____   9. polyvinyl chloride

_____   10. polyurethane

_____   11. polyethylene

_____   12. polystyrene

A. used for millwork
B. feel and fabricating characteristics of real wood
C. used for vapor barriers for construction
D. almost indestructible; can make almost exact reproduction of an original wood pattern
E. highly resistant to impact; stands up to temperature extremes
F. used to imitate wood for ornamentations; stands up well under ordinary use
G. used for see-through furniture

(Continued on next page)

Tell whether each of the following is thermoplastic or thermosetting plastic.

———————————————— 13. polyurethane

———————————————— 14. polyvinyl chloride

———————————————— 15. acrylic

———————————————— 16. laminated plastics

———————————————— 17. polystyrene

———————————————— 18. ABS plastics

Unit 69
DESIGN AND PROCESSES

(Text pages 941-953)

_____ 1. ____ plastics are used for see-through Contemporary style furniture.

_____ 2. ____ plastic is a durable, impact-resistant material that has a glossy "wet look" surface and comes in a wide range of colors.

_____ 3. Which of the following types of plastic is *not* generally used to imitate wood?
A. polystyrene
B. polyester resin
C. polyvinyl chloride
D. polyurethane

_____ 4. What is the most expensive method of forming plastics?

_____ 5. What method is usually used to form polystyrene parts?

_____ 6. The joint usually used to join furniture made of all plastics is the patented ____ joint.

_____ 7. Plastic parts cannot be attached to wood with nails or screws. (True or False)

(Continued on next page)

Identify the processes for manufacturing plastic products.

_____ 8.

_____ 9.

_____ 10.

_____ 11.

_____ 12.

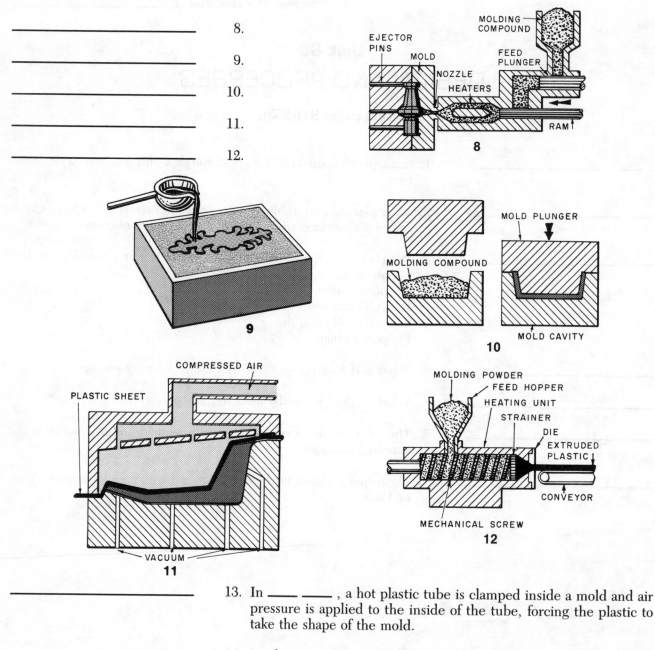

13. In ___ ___ , a hot plastic tube is clamped inside a mold and air pressure is applied to the inside of the tube, forcing the plastic to take the shape of the mold.

14. In the ___ ___ method of forming plastics, a plastic resin is placed on the inside of a metal mold and then the mold is rotated in an oven.

15. ___ plastics are made up of layers of plastic materials and paper bonded together by heat and pressure.

Unit 70
WORKING WITH ACRYLIC PLASTICS

(Text pages 953-962)

_____   1. Acrylic plastics are thermosetting plastics. (True or False)

_____   2. Acrylic plastics have excellent resistance to weathering, so they can be used both indoors and outdoors. (True or False)

_____   3. Acrylics are lighter weight than both glass and aluminum. (True or False)

_____   4. Acrylics should be stored
    A. flat.
    B. horizontally on edge.
    C. vertically on edge.
    D. in a warm place.

_____   5. Masking paper should be removed from the acrylic sheet before any cutting operations are performed. (True or False)

_____   6. _____ teeth are best suited for production work when cutting acrylics with the circular saw.

_____   7. Hollow-ground blades are very good for cutting plastics. (True or False)

_____   8. For cutting plastics with portable power saws, use _____ _____ _____ blades.

_____   9. Blades on table saws should be raised at least _____ inch(es) above the surface of the table when cutting acrylics.

_____   10. What type band saw blade should be used for cutting acrylics?

_____   11. How many teeth per inch should the band saw blade have?

_____   12. Jig and saber saw blades should have _____ teeth per inch when cutting acrylics.

_____   13. The scraping tool for edge finishing acrylic sheets after they have been cut should have a knife edge. (True or False)

_____   14. When drilling plastic, always place it over a(n) _____ _____ and clamp or hold it firmly.

(Continued on next page)

_____ 15. Drill plastics at a high speed. (True or False)

_____ 16. To bend an acrylic sheet along a straight line use a(n) ____ ____ .

_____ 17. The heating element should be applied directly to the plastic. (True or False)

_____ 18. Keep the side heated ____ on the outside of the bend.

_____ 19. Remove masking paper from the acrylic before beginning bending operations. (True or False)

_____ 20. Wear ____ ____ when handling heated plastics.

_____ 21. Bending material before it is thoroughly heated results in ____ ____ along the bend.

_____ 22. Line bending should not be done on sheets more than ____ thick.

_____ 23. Compound curves are made by placing a uniformly heated acrylic sheet over or in a(n) ____ .

_____ 24. To uniformly heat the acrylic, use a large ____ ____ .

_____ 25. Each kind of plastic has a different forming temperature range. (True or False)

_____ 26. A sheet is heated 10 to 20 minutes for each ____ of thickness.

_____ 27. Before heating acrylic for this operation, clean it with a soft, clean cloth dampened with ____ .

_____ 28. Minor scratches and saw marks are removed from acrylic by ____ .

_____ 29. If two acrylic parts fit together perfectly, they can be joined with ____ cement.

_____ 30. Before cementing, the surfaces to be joined should be sanded but not polished. (True or False)

_____ 31. What type screws should be used for fastening acrylics?

_____ 32. When using screws to fasten plastics, oversized holes should be drilled. (True or False)

Unit 71
WORKING WITH FIBER-REINFORCED PLASTICS

(Text pages 962-967)

_____

1. Which of the following is *not* a characteristic of fiber-reinforced plastics?
   A. Even thin pieces are very strong.
   B. It is antistatic.
   C. Front and back surfaces are very smooth.
   D. It can be joined to wood or metal without danger of cracking.

_____

2. The two major ingredients in fiber-reinforced plastic products are fiberglass and a liquid laminating plastic called ____ ____ .

_____

3. A ____ is mixed with the liquid laminating plastic to make it harden.

_____

4. The mold cavity must be coated with a ____ ____ to keep the molded part from sticking to it.

_____

5. Solvents made of ____ are used to clean brushes and other materials used when making fiber-reinforced plastics.

_____

6. You should wear rubber gloves when making fiber-reinforced plastics. (True or False)

_____

7. Wear a ____ when sanding a fiberglass surface.

_____

8. If the surface of the pattern is wood, it must be sealed, primed, and given three coats of
   A. polyurethane.
   B. varnish.
   C. shellac.
   D. lacquer.

_____

9. To keep a wood pattern from sticking to the mold, apply three coats of ____ ____ .

_____

10. First apply the ____ ____ , which is a specially formulated liquid plastic containing a filler material.

_____

11. The purpose of this first coat is to provide the part with a smooth, decorative, and durable surface. (True or False)

_____

12. The fiberglass cloth or mat should be ____ at the corners or at complex curves where wrinkles might appear.

(Continued on next page)

13. Fiberglass cloth must be one continuous piece cut to fit the mold, not sections fitted together. (True or False)

14. An indication that the fiberglass cloth is thoroughly saturated is when
    A. the cloth turns completely white.
    B. bubbles appear on the surface.
    C. the cloth will accept no more liquid plastic.
    D. the cloth becomes transparent.

15. To press out any entrapped air, use a squeegee or roller and work from one edge to the other. (True or False)

16. How many layers of fiberglass and liquid plastic are usually needed for small decorative products?

17. Approximately how thick should a chair seat of fiber-reinforced plastics be?

18. If the laminate is to be very thick, layers must be applied in stages, not one right after the other. (True or False)

19. After the last layer has been applied, allow the unit to cure at least ___ ___ .

20. What should be used to trim any excess plastic along the edges?

21. Sand the entire surface with No. ___ wet-dry abrasive cloth.

Unit 72
CASTING URETHANE FOAM PARTS

(Text pages 967-979)

_____ 1. Urethane foam should be used only for decorative parts, not structural parts such as legs. (True or False)

_____ 2. Buy all foam ingredients for making urethane foam from the same manufacturer to make sure they are compatible. (True or False)

_____ 3. Casting parts of urethane foam is much like casting metal parts. (True or False)

_____ 4. The flexible mold-making compound consists of a catalyst and a(n) _____ .

_____ 5. ____ ____ is needed to fill imperfections in the pattern and seal the box that will hold the pattern and mold.

_____ 6. Make the box from ____ ____ .

_____ 7. For school-shop use, a brush-on mold release is preferred. (True or False)

_____ 8. Resins should be stored in a cool place. (True or False)

_____ 9. Leave _____ clearance space between the pattern and the sides and the top of the mold box.

_____ 10. Use ____ ____ for fillers to seal off areas in the mold box where clearances between box and pattern are too large.

_____ 11. When making the mold, the box should have a lid with _____ holes drilled every 25 square inches.

_____ 12. Apply ____ ____ to the back of the pattern to fasten it to the bottom of the mold box.

_____ 13. You have filled the mold too full if some of the mold mixture bleeds out through the holes when the lid is placed on. (True or False)

_____ 14. Remove the mold from the box after ____ ____ .

_____ 15. Strip the mold from the pattern, not the pattern from the mold. (True or False)

(Continued on next page)

_____

16. The mold is ready to use as soon as the pattern has been removed. (True or False)

_____

17. Use the same box and lid for the casting process that you used when making the mold. (True or False)

_____

18. A ____ ____ is applied to the mold cavity to allow the urethane foam to receive wood stains and finishes.

_____

19. If possible, preheat the mold before pouring in the foam. (True or False)

_____

20. Place a thin piece of ____ ____ over the top of the urethane foam to allow gases to escape during curing.

_____

21. The lid must be clamped on. (True or False)

_____

22. The cast part can be removed after ____ ____ .

_____

23. The foam part achieves its full strength after ____ ____ .

_____

24. When mixing Silastic silicone rubber for a mold material, the ingredients should be thoroughly beaten or whipped until they are a uniform color. (True or False)

_____

25. When using a silicone rubber mold to cast plaster of paris, a mold box is not needed. (True or False)